Jamie Buckingham

TEN BIBLE PEOPLE LIKE ME
WORKBOOK

Ten Character Studies of Bible People Like Me
To be used with "Ten Bible People Like Me" Video Series

10 Bible People Like Me Workbook
By Jamie Buckingham

Published by Risky Living Ministries, Inc.
3901 Hield Road NW
Palm Bay, Florida, 32907
www.rlmin.com

Risky Living Ministries is dedicated to preserving the life works of Jamie Buckingham.

Cover Photo by Bruce Buckingham

ISBN: 978-1494465636

Ten Bible People Like Me
WORKBOOK

TEN BIBLE PEOPLE LIKE ME
by
Jamie Buckingham

CONTENTS

Ten Bible People Like Me

1. God loves ordinary people.
2. All God is looking for is someone willing to obey.
3. God uses whom He chooses.
4. There are no big and no little people in God's eyes.
5. Bible people were just like me.

Ten Bible People Like Me

INTRODUCTION
Read This First

The men and women of the Bible were no different from the men and women of today. Customs were different. The culture was different. They did not have modern transportation, communication, or military machinery. But inside, they were people like us. They had the same appetites, struggled with the same problems and temptations, had the same bodies, the same emotions, and the same loves. Their relationship with God was no better, and no worse, than ours.

In this workbook you will look at ten of these people. Each of them struggled with the same problems you struggle with. Abraham struggled with obeying God. Joshua had tough decisions to make as he went against the crowd. David had to learn from his mistakes. And John Mark, three times a failure, finally made it as a winner.

I am in debt to each of these people. Each has taught me something. Recently, when I was struggling with a major decision in my life, I went to Israel and stood where Abraham stood when he allowed his worthless nephew Lot to inhabit the green pastures of the Jordan, leaving only the desert hills for Abraham to feed his flocks. I saw how God had blessed Abraham because of his willingness to lay down his right to be right. I returned home, and made a similar decision in my life.

On another occasion, feeling I had made a mess of my life, I followed the life of John Mark through the pages of the New Testament. Here I found a young man who always started out strong, but let people down when it really counted. I saw where I had done that to others. But because John Mark's heart was right, God honored him. John Mark's story gave me courage to keep trying.

When our church was going through a tough struggle, and some folks were leaving, I learned a lesson from Gideon. Standing at the "Springs of Gideon," I was reminded of how God weeded Gideon's army down from its original size of 33,000 to only 300 men. But that's all it took to defeat the dreaded Midianite foe. Sheer numbers, I learned from Gideon, mean nothing. God, like the U.S. Marine Corps, is simply looking for a few good men.

Because of what I had learned from the men and women of the Bible, I decided to share their lives with others. In the fall of 1987 I visited Israel with a video camera crew. I went to ten sites where these people lived. I went far north, near the border of Lebanon, where—in a place surrounded by heathen temples—Jesus asked Peter, "Who do you say I am?"

"Thou art the Christ, the son of the Living God," Peter answered.

Looking around at the temple ruins, I realized how tough it was to hear God.

I stood above the plain of Armageddon where Deborah risked her life to save her nation.

I walked through the deep wadi, or canyon, where Elijah lived when he was fed by the ravens. A rushing wall of water had just roared through that dried river bed the night before, picking up speed as it cascaded downhill all the way to the Dead Sea. In the bottom of the canyon, unearthed by the water the night before, I discovered an unexploded hand grenade. It was a grim reminder of the wars still being fought over that tiny bit of land.

I rested in the shade of a huge tree beside the Jordan River where John the Baptist baptized Jesus.

And one evening I sat beside a sparkling spring in the tiny village of Ein Karem, just south of Jerusalem. I realized it was probably there, where the water from the spring flowed down into an ancient vineyard, that the Holy Spirit impregnated a frightened, but totally submitted, young virgin named Mary.

Standing on the sites where these men and women had their great experiences, I video-taped the brief messages which accompany these lessons.

This workbook has been designed to be used with those taped video messages. The workbook will be best used in a small group of people who have a leader (teacher or instructor). Ideal usage calls for the same group to meet once a week for ten weeks. You'll need your Bible, because the questions in the workbook are all taken from the various scriptural accounts of Jesus' parables—plus a number of related passages. Each session should last about an hour and should begin as the group views the section of the video tape pertaining to the chapter to be studied. Each video segment runs about 12 minutes. Then the teacher will take over, using this workbook as a guide, and lead the class in a study of the material at hand.

When this material was first produced, some people complained that the video teaching segments were not long enough. They were accustomed to lengthy teaching videos—talking heads preaching sermons from the tube. However, I believe that while video is an important teaching tool (you could never see what I saw without it), it is not a substitute for the personalization brought by a teacher, a workbook, and a Bible.

What I have given you is the best of both methods.

Several years ago I produced a similar set of video tapes and a workbook called "The Journey to Spiritual Maturity." In it, I traced the footsteps of Moses through the Sinai, pausing to teach along the way. Shortly after that material was distributed, I began getting letters from prison and jail chaplains—as well as Bible study leaders who were working with men and women behind bars. They were saying the material was ideal for prison Bible studies since it combined the visual (video) with the written (workbook) with an instructor. Video alone is not sufficient to convey truth. It must be combined with the personal touch of a teacher to answer—and ask—questions, and a workbook to stimulate actual Bible reading and study.

Encouraged that prisoners were using the material, I prepared three more series using the same technique. One series covered "Ten Miracles of Jesus." Another studied "Ten Parables of Jesus." Both were done on location in Israel. This is the third of those series, which looks at "Ten Bible People Like Me." All were originally designed to be used in prisons and jails where hundreds of thousands of men and women are eagerly learning more about God.

However, it soon became evident that what is good for prisoners is good for all. Therefore I modified the material so it can be used just as easily by a Sunday school class or a home group as by a prison Bible study group.

As you study the lives of these ordinary people, you will discover how they did extraordinary things because they submitted to God. As Longfellow said:

> Lives of great men all remind us
> We can make our lives sublime,
> And, departing, leave behind us
> Footprints on the sands of time.

The same Holy Spirit Who inspired and empowered these men and women will give you inspiration and power as well. The purpose of this workbook is to stimulate you, excite you, and change you by bringing you to the place where you will see that the stories of the people in the Bible were not just for yesterday—they are for today. They were not just for those people of distant lands and times—they are for you.

In this study you will visit with me the places where these Bible people lived. You'll see the ruins of ancient Jericho where the walls fell as Joshua and his army marched around them. You'll see a magnificent wild ibex standing high above the Dead Sea near the place where God sent a ram for Abraham to sacrifice in place of sacrificing his son, Isaac. You'll see the area where John the Baptist lived in the wilderness, eating locusts and wild honey. And you'll come with me at night to the Garden of Gethsemane where young John Mark, only a teenager, fled into the darkness—afraid to stand up for Jesus when the soldiers came to arrest Him.

But once the video is off, the real fun begins. It is then you will open your Bible and begin to study the lives of these people for yourself. Not just to learn what they said—but to discover what God is saying to you from their struggles, mistakes, and victories.

Are you like Mary, frightened but submitted? Maybe you're struggling with decisions like Abraham. Perhaps, like David, you're having to learn from your mistakes. Or maybe, like Deborah, you're having to learn to trust people to help you out in tough times.

As I said, you'll meet yourself in every one of these people. And hopefully, the person you see will then call out to God for change and growth.

If you are hungry and thirsty for righteousness, studying the lives of these people will enable you to see yourself in a new way. They, in turn, will introduce you to the One who has the power to change you. And He will be so attractive you'll rush to invite Him into your life in a new way.

Welcome to the wonderful world of the Bible. Meet ten Bible people who are just like you.

Jamie Buckingham
Melbourne, Florida

GETTING THE MOST FROM THIS STUDY

Using the accompanying video tapes, this workbook is designed to lead you, step by step, into the lives of ten Bible people just like you. The video segments of these lessons were taped on the locations in Israel where these people lived. You will see the Jordan River where John baptized Jesus, the plain of Armageddon where Deborah won a decisive victory—and where tradition says the last battle of history will be fought before Jesus returns. You'll go with me into a deep, mysterious, wadi (canyon) in the Judean wilderness where the ravens—still abundant in Israel—fed Elijah. You will be as much a part of the audience as the group of people who accompanied the camera crew when the tapes were made.

These Bible people are still speaking to the hearts of all those who have "ears to hear," as Jesus was fond of saying. It is my prayer that as you study their lives in your Bible and answer the questions in this workbook, you, too, will allow God's Spirit to speak directly to your heart—even as He spoke to Abraham, Mary, and Peter. He is still speaking, and if you allow Him, He will change your entire outlook, giving you a new quality of life and ministry on earth.

The material on the video tape and in this workbook can be used in a number of different ways. It can be the basis of an individual study. It can be used in a small group, such as a Bible study group, a Sunday school class, or a house group. Experience has shown the greatest benefit will come when a group of people study the material together under a leader who is well-prepared on the subject.

Helps for the Leader

If you are a leader preparing to take a group of people into a study of Bible people, you should consider the following:

Necessary Materials

A good color television set with a screen large enough to be seen by all present.

A reliable video player.

A power source within reach of the plugs for the TV and VCR.

Comfortable seating so each person may see the TV screen and the teacher.

A Bible for each student. The workbook uses Scripture quotes from the New International Version (NIV), but any Bible will do.

* A workbook for each student.

* Pen or pencil for each student.

2. Preparation

Before teaching others you should not only view the entire video series—all 10 segments—but you should work your way through this workbook. You will find a number of Scripture references. Study them in depth before attempting to lead the class in discussion. You are not expected to have all the answers. Your job will be to help the students ask the right questions and stimulate them to explore the Bible for themselves.

3. Be Aware

As you lead the class, be aware that each person present is going through some kind of crisis in his or her life similar to the ones experienced by each of these Bible people. This could be a financial crisis, a grief experience, a problem with personal identification, a battle with demons or temptation, a crisis in the home, spiritual confusion, or a number of different mountains which seem too high to climb and too thick to tunnel through. Some, like Joshua, will be struggling with whether to follow the crowd or stand alone. Others, like David, want to learn from their mistakes. There will be those needing the courage of John the Baptist. Many will be like John Mark, whom the world labeled a loser. Your awareness of their special needs will help when it comes to answering questions and leading in discussion. Do not be afraid to pause at any place in the discussion and minister to that person or persons—asking the class to join in as the Holy Spirit applies the truth of God to the lives of those who have "ears to hear."

4. Stick to the Subject

Your job as teacher is to hold the discussion to the subject being taught. There will always be those in the class who will want to lead you on some rabbit chase down a side path, will want to monopolize the discussion, or try to entice you into an argument over some minor point. It is important you stick, as nearly as possible, to the outline of the subject at hand. The material has been carefully designed to build principle on principle, with the eventual aim of the student becoming "thoroughly equipped for every good work" (II Timothy 3:17). Do not preach. Do not monopolize the conversation yourself. Do not allow the class to drift from the subject matter.

5. Stimulate Discussion

Remember, your job as teacher is not to give answers—even if you know them—but to skillfully stimulate discussion and encourage each student to find God's Word for his own life. The Holy Spirit will help you, for He not only wants each student to understand the truths discovered by these Bible people, He wants each one to let the life-changing truth of each story bring him to a place of resolution. Do not limit yourself to the material covered in this workbook. It is merely a guide, a primer for discussion. Allow the Holy Spirit to direct your class sessions.

6. Be Sensitive to Time

If your class has more than an hour for each study, arrange for a break of a few minutes for refreshment or a stretch. If the group discussion is dynamic, or if someone in the class indicates a need for personal ministry, you may want to keep the session going. Or, if the particular subject stimulates extra discussion, you may want to put off the next segment in order to continue that one for an additional week. For instance, the study of the principles in Lesson 5—"David: Learning From Your Mistakes"—can hardly be contained in one session. The same is true of Lesson 4—"Gideon: Doing Things God's Way." If that is the case, I recommend the class review the same video segment at the opening of the second week of study to stimulate continuing discussion.

Remember, just because the class has ended does not mean the Holy Spirit will not continue to work. In fact, in all probability the greatest work of the Spirit in the lives of the students will take place after the class is over. That means you may want to open the next class with a brief report on the Spirit's activity since the class last met.

Helps for Students

Before you start this course, ask yourself these questions:

* Am I really committed to finding God's will for my life?

* Am I willing to commit myself to attend all the sessions of this course unless unavoidably detained?

* Am I willing to open my mind to new truth beyond what I now believe?

* Am I willing to prepare ahead of time through prayer and by reading my Bible and doing the work in my workbook?

* Am I willing to enter into the group discussion—asking questions and expressing my personal opinions?

* Am I willing, if I think God is prodding me, to ask for personal ministry?

* Am I willing, if someone else expresses a need, to be used by God to speak today's truth into that person's life, just as Jesus spoke 2000 years ago?

If you answered "no" to any of these questions, you may want to reconsider whether you should take this course. You are getting ready to touch the Word of God, and to examine the heart of God's truth. You should not enter into this course lightly or unadvisedly. Once you begin a serious study of Bible people, God, in all likelihood, will begin to teach you personally—about things in your life which need to be changed. If you are not ready for that to happen, you may want to sit this one out.

On the other hand, if you answered "yes" to the questions, you are ready to proceed. Here are some immediate steps you can take to insure maximum benefit from the course.

1. Set Goals

This course is designed not only to introduce you to these ten Bible people, but to introduce you to God in a new and exciting way. It does not matter whether you are young or old, a seasoned Christian or just a seeker. God still speaks to anyone who will listen. Like the rain, which falls on the just and the unjust, God loves to reveal himself to all who reach out to Him. The principles learned over these next several class sessions will help you, first of all, to understand the lessons learned by these Bible people. But, more important, they will lead you to the place where the same Holy Spirit who revealed God to Simon Peter will reveal Him to you. Look ahead to what you need—and what kind of person you want to be. Do you want to be a better person? Do you want to think—and act—like a man or woman of God? Set a goal and let this study help you get there.

2. Honestly Evaluate Your Present Condition

What are your needs—your real needs? A prisoner may feel his primary need is to be free. On the other hand, remember, Jesus said the greater bondage is the bondage of the soul and spirit. Studying the lives of these Bible people will open the prison doors of your soul—allowing your spirit to soar free with joy and power.

Honestly evaluate your present condition as you begin to study the lives of these people, for without a willingness to face yourself, it will be extremely difficult to understand what God is saying to you concerning your past, present, and future.

Your faith commitment to dig into the Bible and examine the nature of God and his Kingdom must be accompanied by constant self-measurement and self-inventory. You know the kind of person you already are. You know the level of commitment you already display. You know your faith level. The question you must now face is: "Am I willing to allow the awesome truths discovered by these people to change my life?"

At the end of each chapter there is a place where you—in the privacy of your own study—can evaluate your personal progress. The answers you give to the questions will give you a spiritual indicator of your progress week by week. The questions will also help fix the Word of God more firmly in your heart, and thus provide a reservoir of truth that the Holy Spirit can draw upon in the training and reshaping of your life until you are conformed to the image of Jesus.

3. You'll Not Pass This Way Again

Although God gives each man and woman infinite chances to improve and move into spiritual maturity, there are certain times when miracles are offered—and if refused, are not offered again. Thus, when discussion in class opens the door for you to express yourself, or ask for personal prayer, do not hesitate to respond. One of the things you will be doing during these sessions is learning to hear God—just as Jesus did.

When Joshua and Caleb came back after spying out the Promised Land, they found themselves in the minority. All the other spies said, "We can't do it." But Joshua and Caleb wanted to "go in and possess the land," as God had told them. The others were so opposed to that idea they threatened to kill them. It was a tough time. For Joshua and Caleb it meant going against the crowd. But their willingness to risk all by standing up for what was right allowed God to bless them in ways they never dreamed.

When Peter, dozing on a rooftop in Joppa, saw a vision of a sheet full of non-kosher food being lowered from Heaven, and He heard God's voice say, "Take and eat," he knew God was preparing him for something much bigger than his Jewish mind had ever conceived. But he was ready for whatever God had in store.

That is my prayer for you—that as you study the lives of these people, you will be willing to go against the crowd and be ready for whatever God has in store.

I urge you, therefore, to hear God—and do what He tells you to do, regardless of how illogical it may seem at the time. Only those who seek help find it. Only those who are open to truth receive it.

4. Study Each Chapter Before Class

Ideally, you should study each chapter in this workbook before coming to class. Look up each Scripture reference and answer all the questions by filling in the blanks and circling the true/false answers. Of course, if it is impossible to study ahead of time, you should still take part in the class activities.

5. Set Your Own Pace

One of the lessons you will learn as you study the Bible is this: God's patience is infinite as long as you are moving toward Him. The only time you will begin to feel pressure is when you close your mind, dig in your heels, or get off God's trail by pursuing false ideas and concepts. Do not be afraid to move slowly. To rush through this study may mean you learn all the right religious answers, but miss the Holy Spirit Who is the One who brings miracles today. This course is designed to provoke you to do your own searching, thinking, and praying—and to demonstrate your faith in God.

6. Check Your Progress

Once you have completed the course, ask your chaplain, pastor, or group leader to sit down with you and review where you are in life. Remember the statement Jesus often made: "Those with ears to hear, let them hear."

7. Finally

Unless otherwise stated, Scripture quotations are taken from the New International Version (NIV) of the Bible, copyright 1978 by New York International Bible Society and published by Zondervan Corporation, Grand Rapids, Michigan, used by permission. Each chapter has a number of questions with accompanying Scripture references. By looking up the references you should be able to answer all the questions. Do not be afraid to fill in the blanks—even if you give the wrong answer. No one is going to grade you. This course is like those wonderful Special Olympics for handicapped children—everyone who enters is called a winner, regardless of how he finishes.

You will be awarded a Certificate of Completion at the end of the course, signed by me and your instructor. All you have to do is finish. That makes you a winner. By looking up the answers in the Bible you will learn. Go ahead, try it. It's fun to learn—especially when you are learning about God.

As you study the lives and struggles of these Bible people, you will begin to understand that each one was simply a person like you. Each one was fighting his own personal battles. David had a problem with his wife. Gideon was afraid. Mary was faced with an impossible situation. John Mark had been branded a loser. But in the end, each one became a winner.

That's God's wonderful promise to you. You, too, can be a winner. An overcomer.

The purpose of this workbook, along with the accompanying video tape series, is to bring you to that place of victory. Regardless of your circumstances, one man, with God, makes a majority. And remember, the only thing more exciting than studying how God worked in the lives of these people is letting God work in your life. Bible people are not the only winners in life. God wants you to be a winner, too.

Jamie Buckingham

Lesson 1

Abraham

Making the Tough Decisions

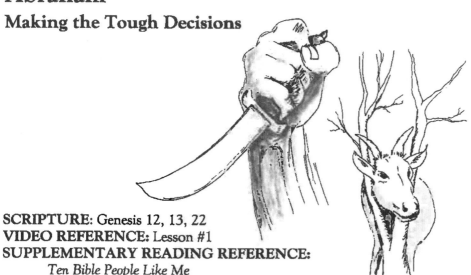

SCRIPTURE: Genesis 12, 13, 22
VIDEO REFERENCE: Lesson #1
SUPPLEMENTARY READING REFERENCE:
    Ten Bible People Like Me
    Chapter I: "Abraham: Making the Tough Decisions"

1. The Call of God

The first man to experience a "call" from God was Abram—later called Abraham. In the days and centuries to follow, many others would be called by God to perform specific tasks. Some would be called to follow God for whatever task God had in mind. All would be called to walk out that call by faith.

The pattern was first set by God's call on Abram, however.

What did God call Abram to do? (Genesis 12:1)

to leave his native country

Terah, Abram's father, had moved his family from Ur, near the border of Iran in Iraq, to a place called Haran in what is now southern Turkey. After Terah died, God called Abram.

Whom did Abram take with him when he left Haran? (Genesis 12:5)

1. his wife, Sarai
2. nephew, Lot
3. all his wealth - livestock etc.

List seven things God promised Abram before he left Haran. (Genesis 12:2-3)

1. I will make you into a great nation
2. I will bless you and make you famous
3. I will bless you and your families.

11

Old Testament-
holy spirit visited
to give a 'call'
New Testament-
post Jesus HS lives
in us - discernment
me? HS? Satan?

4. _____

5. _____

6. _____

7. _____

_____

What did God promise Abram after he arrived in Canaan? (Genesis 12:7)

_____

Two thousand years after Abraham left his homeland to follow God, the writer of Hebrews lists him in his "line-up of heroes."

What single character trait of Abraham's is remembered as the central strength of his life? (Hebrews 11:8)

_____ His love of family

_____ His personal wealth

_____ His influence in the nation

_____ His dedication as a father

_____ His obedience to God

Many of the people listed in the Bible received specific instructions from God as they started out in ministry.

What did God tell Noah to do? (Genesis 6:14)

_____

_____

Where did God tell Jacob to go? (Genesis 35:1)

_____

_____

Where was Moses to go and what was he to do? (Exodus 3:7-10)

_____

_____

What specific instructions did God give to Joshua? (Joshua 1:1-2)

_____

_____

Abraham, however, did not receive specific instructions. He was to walk by faith, rather than by sight.

Where was Abraham told to go? (Hebrews 11:8)

_____

_____

How much direction did Abraham have? (Hebrews 11:8)

_____ God told him not to start out until he knew where he was going.

_____ He started out not knowing where he was going.

2. The Covenant

In Stephen's sermon to the Sanhedrin—a sermon which so angered the Jewish leaders they stoned him to death—he reminded the officials of Abram's obedience to God.

How much land did God give to Abram? (Acts 7:5)

_____

_____

Abram owned no land, but simply moved his herds from one area to another. After visiting Egypt he returned to Canaan and allowed his flocks to graze in the rich, green Jordan Valley at the northern end of the Dead Sea.

As is often the case, each new act of faith and surrender was met with a challenge. No sooner had his heart been set right with God than a fresh testing confronted him—strife in his own clan. Abram's worthless nephew, Lot, was not satisfied. He not only wanted the pasture for himself, he wanted to live near the exciting cities of Sodom and Gomorrah along the Dead Sea.

Abram had other priorities, however. He was not called to be a settler; he was called to be a pioneer.

What was Abram called? (Genesis 14:13)

the Hebrew— wanderer, nomad

The term "Hebrew" means wanderer, pilgrim, nomad. Thus, when Lot said there was not room enough for the two of them, Abram chose once again to obey God. Jealous for the integrity of his tribe and its testimony before the corrupt society which was so closely observing him, he determined he should not dishonor God by causing disunity and conflict within his family—a family who had professed a loyalty to God, making them different from the pagans.

Where did Abram wind up when he left Lot? (Genesis 13:18)

Oak grove belonging to Mamre

What did he do after he arrived? (Genesis 13:18)

he built an altar to the Lord

Where you locate your family is important to their salvation. Lot chose to live where he could find pleasure, and did not give consideration to the spiritual danger he was causing his family. He failed to see that his selfishness, which led to a prayerless, hasty, carnal choice, would lead to disaster down the road. He should have been aware of the results of his bad choice.

Where did Lot pitch his tents? (Genesis 13:12)

near Sodom

What kind of people lived in Sodom? (Genesis 13:13)

unusually wicked

What became of Lot's wife? (Genesis 19:15-17, 24-26)

turned to a pillar of salt

What became of Lot's daughters? (Genesis 19:30-33, 36)

they slept with their father

The two children produced by the incestuous relationship between Lot and his daughters were the founders of two warring tribes—the Moabites and the Ammonites—who across history remained enemies of God's people, the Israelites. Such were the results of Lot's choice to disobey God.

How did God reward Abram for his obedience? (Genesis 13:14-17)

He gave him all the land and he promised to give him descendants as numerous as the dust

God had tested Abram to see if he would obey. Abram passed with flying colors. Now God knew that Abram would not only obey Him regarding his business, but regarding his family as well.

What did God say He had discovered about Abram as a father? (Genesis 18:19)

He will direct his sons and families to do what is write

The Bible says God rewards those who obey Him in the tough decisions.

What four things did God tell the children of Israel to do? (Exodus 15:26)

1. listen to Gods voice
2. do what is right in gods sight
3. keep his commands
4. _____

What did God promise the children of Israel He would do if they obeyed Him? (Exodus 15:26)

No diseases

How did God reward Caleb for obedience? (Numbers 14:24)

He got his full share of the land

How did God reward Joshua for obedience? (Joshua 1:3)

he was given land

What did God promise Solomon if he would obey Him? (I Kings 3:14)

long life

Whom did Peter and the apostles say they had to obey? (Acts 5:29)

God, rather than man

Whose presence do you have if you obey the teachings of Jesus? (II John 9)

Father + Son

3. The Final Test

As Abram grew old (his name was now changed to Abraham) he began to doubt. Could God really be trusted, he wondered? In Genesis 20 we find him falling back into the old sin of distrust. God chastises him, and he repents.

God had promised Abraham that He would bless his children, that they would become as numerous as the sand on the seashore and the stars in the sky. But Abraham and his wife, Sarah, had only one child—a boy named Isaac. That son was the child through whom the covenant of God would come to pass.

Then God spoke once more to Abraham, telling him to do something so unthinkable, so horrible, that any normal man would have balked. It was a final test. But across the years Abraham had learned he could trust God, no matter how strange the request.

This time the request seemed beyond reason.

What did God tell Abraham to do? (Genesis 22:2)

take your son up to sacrafice

How did Abraham respond? (Genesis 22:3)

he went up to the mtn

What did Abraham tell his two servants? (Genesis 22:5)

Stay here - WE will return

Even though God had told Abraham to sacrifice his son, Isaac, as a burnt offering, Abraham had faith to believe God had something better in mind. Abraham knew God, and knew God would not require him to kill his son. That was not the nature of God. All Abraham could do was obey, however, and trust God to show him something he had not yet seen.

When Abraham and Isaac left the servants to climb to the top of Mt. Moriah, whom did Abraham tell the servants would return? (Genesis 22:5)

_____ He would return alone.

_____ An angel would return with him.

___X___ He and Isaac would return.

When Isaac asked his father about the lamb for the burnt offering, how did Abraham reply? (Genesis 22:8)

God will provide the Lamb

How much did Abraham have to do before God stopped him? (Genesis 22:9-10)

1. Built alter
2. Arranged wood
3. Bound the son
4. Laid him on alter
5. took the knife

How did God know Abraham could be trusted? (Genesis 22:12)

He did withhold his only son

Abraham had told Isaac that the Lord would provide the lamb for the sacrifice.

How did God do that? (Genesis 22:13)

He provided a ram in the thicket

What did God tell Abraham would happen because Abraham had obeyed? (Genesis 22:18)

I will bless you and multiply your descendants

Who did Jesus say were His friends? (John 15:14)

those that kept his commds

What is the command of Jesus that we are to obey? (John 15:17)

Love one another.

WRAP UP

Abraham had discovered the only way to qualify to receive God's blessing is to obey Him. There are some who feel they should obey because God blesses them. Abraham teaches us that blessings follow obedience.

FINAL LESSON

Obeying God is the only way to please Him.

PERSONAL REVIEW QUESTIONS

Circle T (true) or F (false)

1. T **F** God never calls people to do unpleasant things.

2. T **F** God never calls us to do anything which upsets our present way of living.

3. T **F** God never calls us to do anything without giving us enough sight in advance to walk it out.

4. **T** F God is looking for men and women who will obey Him.

5. T **F** It's always easy to obey God.

6. T **F** God always gives His obedient servants the greenest pastures.

7. **T** F God always blesses those who obey him, even though the blessing may be different than what we expected.

8. T **F** Once God has made a promise to us, He never tests us again.

9. **T** F God always tests those whom He loves.

10. **T** F The purpose of testing is to stretch our faith so we will be more like God.

MEMORY VERSE

John 15:14 (Memorize, then write it on these lines.)

You are my friends if you do
what I command

NOTES

Lesson 2

Joshua
Going Against the Crowd

SCRIPTURE: Joshua 6, 10, Numbers 13-14
VIDEO REFERENCE: Lesson #2
SUPPLEMENTARY READING REFERENCE:
> *Ten Bible People Like Me*
> "Chapter II: "Joshua: Going Against the Crowd"

1. Making Choices

It's tough to make choices, especially when your choice is unpopular—when you have to go against the crowd. Joshua was a man continually faced with choices. Most of those choices went against popular opinion.

Joshua was Moses' second-in-command. Moses met him in Egypt before the Exodus began and immediately saw that Joshua was a born leader. Not only was he a leader, however—he also understood the principle of submission. He never once coveted Moses' position. He was content to be a loyal assistant—standing with Moses when it was not the popular thing to do.

The time was 1200 years before Jesus. The Israelites, who had been slaves in Egypt for more than 400 years, had been set free. Following Moses, they left Egypt and traveled to Mt. Sinai in the southern Sinai peninsula where God gave them a series of laws which would govern them as long as the Jewish race existed. One year after leaving Egypt, the Israelites finally reached the border of Canaan—the promised land. They camped at a place called Kadesh Barnea. Here they re-grouped, paused to be refreshed, and gained strength. Then they were to take that final step of conquest. But something happened. Moses sent 12 spies into the land of Canaan to bring back a report on the condition of the roads, the location of the cities, the morale of the people, the size of the armies, the type of agriculture, and other necessary facts. He chose one man from each of the 12 tribes. Joshua was the representative of the tribe of Ephraim.

When the 12 spies returned, Moses asked for a report. The spies gave them information he had not asked for. Instead of reporting on the land, they reported on the inhabitants of the land. Ten of the spies said it would be impossible to conquer this land—that they ought to go back to Egypt.

Joshua and his friend Caleb from the tribe of Judah, however, went against the crowd. They called on the people to have faith in God's promises rather than look at the circumstances. It was an unpopular vote.

What did the unbelieving Israelites want to do to Joshua and Caleb? (Numbers 14:10)

_____

Joshua and Caleb, however, held their ground. They believed God could be trusted to deliver them from the giants in the land. It was the people who balked. As a result, God told the people they would remain in the wilderness for another 38 years until the entire, untrusting generation had died. Only Joshua and Caleb would live to enter the promised land.

God had promised them the land. He had proven Himself faithful at every turn of their journey up to that point. Joshua knew He could be trusted to go before them and fight their battles for them.

What had God promised the Israelites? (Deuteronomy 1:21)

_____

_____

_____

Instead of listening to God's promises, the Israelites focused on the problems.

Why did the Israelites say they could not attack the Canaanites? (Numbers 13:31)

_____

_____

When the Israelites took their eyes off God and looked at themselves, how did they see themselves? (Numbers 13:33)

_____

_____

2. Unbelief

Unbelief never sees beyond difficulties. It is always looking at walled cities and giants rather than at God. Faith looks at God; unbelief looks at obstacles. The Israelites, when they took their eyes off God, saw themselves as grasshoppers. The more they confessed their inadequacies and inabilities, the more they saw them as reality. Only Joshua and Caleb were willing to do the unpopular thing—call the people to look at God rather than the giants.

Many years later Jesus spoke of this unbelief.

Why was Jesus unable to perform miracles in His hometown? (Matthew 13:58)

_____

On another occasion, Jesus rebuked his followers who said they were powerless to cast a demon out of a child. After Jesus took authority over the demon and commanded it to leave, His disciples asked Him, "Why couldn't we drive it out?"

Why were the disciples powerless? (Matthew 17:20)

_____

How much faith did Jesus say was necessary to move mountains? (Matthew 17:20)

_____

What prevented the Israelites from entering the Promised Land? (Hebrews 3:19)

_____

God rewarded Joshua for his willingness to make correct choices and go against the crowd.

How did God reward Joshua and Caleb? (Numbers 14:30)

_____

3. Jesus and Faith

One time Jesus was stopped by two blind men who called out to Him, asking Him to heal them. When Jesus asked them if they believed He could do it, they said yes, they believed. Jesus then touched their eyes and they received sight.

What did Jesus say qualified them to be healed? (Matthew 9:29)

_____

On another occasion when Jesus was teaching, some men literally removed the roof of the house He was in. They lowered a crippled man down through the ceiling by ropes which were attached to his bed.

What was it that impressed Jesus about this act? (Mark 2:5)

_____

What did Jesus say we would be able to do if we have faith? (John 14:12)

_____

_____

What did Jesus say God would give us if we ask Him in the name of His Son? (John 14:14)

_____

4. Joshua and Faith

Joshua was able to make correct choices because he had faith. After Moses died, Joshua was appointed leader of the Israelites. Now ready to enter the Promised Land, they came to the Jordan River. Before entering Joshua did something Moses had done earlier.

What did Joshua do before invading Canaan? (Joshua 2:1)

_____

While Moses sent 12 spies, how many did Joshua send? (Joshua 2:1)

_____ 144,000

_____ 70 x 7

_____ 666

_____ 2

To whom did Moses' 12 spies report when they returned? (Numbers 13:26)

_____ To Moses alone

_____ To Moses and Aaron

_____ To a military tribunal

_____ To the whole Israelite community

To whom did Joshua's spies report when they returned? (Joshua 2:23-24)

_____ To the whole Israelite community

_____ To the elders of the tribes

_____ To a Congressional subcommittee

_____ To Joshua alone

Moses had asked his spies to report on the entire nation. Joshua was far more specialized, asking his spies to check out the first military objective.

What were the spies instructed to look at? (Joshua 2:1)

_____

Even if the spies had brought back a report that would not have pleased the people, Joshua was prepared to go in and occupy the land.

What had God told Joshua that made him so confident? (Joshua 1:3)

_____

_____

After crossing the river, Joshua told his army to surround the walled city of Jericho.

Who actually led the Israelites into battle? (Joshua 5:13-14)

_____

What strange—and unpopular—procedure did the Lord tell Joshua to use to bring down the walls of Jericho? (Joshua 6:3-5)

_____

_____

_____

_____

Joshua was a man of courage, not because he fought bravely against the enemy, but because he was willing to make unpopular choices. He did not make these choices on the basis of his intellect, however. He listened to God and followed His direction.

What three things does God tell us to do if we expect Him to bless our choices? (Proverbs 3:5-6)

1. _____
2. _____
3. _____

What will God do if we do these three things? (Proverbs 3:5-6)

_____

Paul urged the early Christians, many of whom were dying for their faith, not to follow the ways of the world but to follow God—even if it meant physical death.

What was Paul's attitude about the Gospel? (Romans 1:16)

_____

What choice did Paul tell the Christians they should make concerning their bodies? (Romans 12:1)

_____

_____

How are we to gain strength so we can go against the crowd? (Romans 12:2)

_____

_____

_____

WRAP UP

We learn from Joshua, a man like us, that the correct choices are not always popular. Joshua, though, had been willing to learn from Moses. Because he learned his lesson well, and because he was a man of the Bible, God promised him success. In fact, the only time the word "success" is used in the Bible is in Joshua 1:8, where God told Joshua that if he would do everything written in God's book he would be "prosperous and successful." Success does not come by making popular decisions. It comes by obeying God.

FINAL LESSON

If you are determined to follow the will of God, even your wrong choices will turn out to be right.

PERSONAL REVIEW QUESTIONS

Circle T (true) or F (false)

1. T   F   Joshua was second-in-command to Moses.

2. T   F   On three occasions Joshua rebelled against Moses.

3. T   F   Moses sent 12 spies into the Promised Land.

4. T   F   Only Joshua brought back a positive report.

5. T   F   The people responded positively to Joshua's challenge.

6. T   F   Joshua said the people of Canaan were like giant grasshoppers.

7. T   F   All you need is faith the size of a tiny seed to move mountains.

8. T   F   Joshua also sent 12 spies into the Promised Land.

9. T   F   God says it's foolish to keep on going against public opinion.

10. T   F   If we lean on our own understanding God will give us wisdom.

11. T   F   Trusting in God means leaning on our own understanding.

12. T   F   Leaning on our own understanding **gives us** transformed minds.

MEMORY VERSE

Romans 12:2 (Memorize, then write it on these lines.)

_____

_____

_____

_____

TRUE OR FALSE ANSWERS:

1-T, 2-F, 3-T, 4-F, 5-F, 6-F, 7-T, 8-F, 9-F, 10-F, 11-F, 12-F

NOTES

Lesson 3
Deborah
Just a Housewife

SCRIPTURE: Judges 4-5
VIDEO REFERENCE: Lesson #3
SUPPLEMENTARY READING REFERENCE:
   Ten Bible People Like Me
   Chapter III: "Deborah: Just a Housewife"

1. Introduction

The year was 1150 B.C. Under the leadership of Joshua, the land of Canaan had been occupied by the Israelites. Joshua had parceled out various sections for each tribe to settle. The tribes were descendants of the 12 sons of Jacob, whose name had been changed to Israel.

What were these people called? (Exodus 12:37)

_____

The 12 tribes each settled on the assigned land: Simeon and Judah in the south, Asher in the far north, Issachar, Zebulun and Manasseh in the center.

2. The Judges

Each tribe operated independently. In fact, they often quarreled among themselves and occasionally even went to war with each other. However, their biggest enemies were not each other, but the hostile nations around them.

Name six of the hostile tribes outside the borders of Israel. (Joshua 24:11)

1. _____

2. _____

3. _____

4. _____

5. _____

6. _____

NOTES

The land the Israelites had conquered had once been called Canaan.

Were the Canaanites inside or outside the borders of Israel? (Judges 1:28)

_____ Inside

_____ Outside

It was an age of battle and violence. These former slaves, now trying to farm the land, were forced to spend much of their time battling the enemy forces. Part of the problem lay in the fact the Israelites never did finish the task of occupying the land. There were pockets of resistance throughout the nation. During the twelfth and eleventh centuries the tribes were attacked by enemies on all sides: the kingdoms of Ammon, Edom and Moab to the east of the Jordan, the Midianites from Arabia, the Philistines along the coast, and by the old Canaanite city-states which still remained in power in the new nation of Israel.

When one of these enemies attacked one or several of the tribal areas, the fussing tribes would put aside their differences and band together against the common enemy. A hasty tribal coalition would be formed under a single, powerful leader called a Judge. These national heros were not born leaders. They were recognized by the people because of their physical strength, intellect, or spiritual maturity. When the crisis was over, they invariably returned to their tribe, and the tribes resumed their independent nature.

It was a dark age for Israel, with wide disorganization, tribal discord, and military defeat. Some of the judges were cruel, murderous men. Some were treacherous. Others immoral. Yet we see God working through such men. While most of these primitive characters did little to reflect God's glory, God remained faithful and still protected His people.

Name the twelve judges of Israel.

(Judges 3:9) _____

(Judges 3:15) _____

(Judges 4:4) _____

(Judges 6:12) _____

(Judges 9:3) _____

(Judges 10:1) _____

(Judges 10:3) _____

(Judges 11:4-6) _____

(Judges 12:8) _____

(Judges 12:11) _____

(Judges 12:13) _____

(Judges 13:24) _____

30

The final judge was also classified as a prophet.

Who was the final judge of Israel before the time of the kings? (I Samuel 3:21)

_____

3. Recognition of Leadership

The most unusual, and one of the most effective, judges was a woman named Deborah.

What was Deborah called besides a judge? (Judges 4:4)

_____

What was her husband's name? (Judges 4:4)

_____

Where was she conducting court? (Judges 4:5)

_____

What function did she perform in her role as judge? (Judges 4:5)

_____

_____

During this time, an evil military leader from a Canaanite city was cruelly oppressing the Israelites.

What was the name of the Canaanite miltary commander? (Judges 4:2)

_____

How long had he been oppressing the Israelites? (Judges 4:3)

_____ 5 years

_____ 10 years

_____ 20 years

_____ 40 years

When it became evident the Israelites could no longer tolerate the evil military commander, Sisera, leaders from various tribes came to Deborah for help.

Deborah had none of the normal qualifications given military leaders of the day. She had not trained for many years under Moses. She had no great physical strength like Samson. Just a housewife—yet across the years she gradually became recognized as a woman of great wisdom.

List Deborah's qualifications.

(Judges 4:4) _____

(Judges 4:4) _____

(Judges 4:5) _____

(Judges 5:7) _____

Deborah was, above all, a woman of wisdom. She knew she was no military commander. She was going to need help.

Whom did Deborah call on to help her? (Judges 4:6)

_____

Deborah towers over all the other figures in this story. Barak is a mere shadow beside her. Some are born to lead, others born to follow. Barak seemed to know his role in this situation and was not ambitious to take Deborah's place. In fact, he seems to be a bit fearful and shy, while deferring to Deborah's leadership.

How did Barak honor Deborah? (Judges 4:8)

_____

_____

Deborah, who was gifted as a prophet, made it clear that God was going to do something different, something the Israelites had never seen before.

What did Deborah prophesy God was going to do? (Judges 4:9)

_____

_____

4. Military Victory

It was a terrifying situation. The Canaanite city of Hazor was a major stronghold. Sisera had taken full advantage of the iron age to develop new weapons and armor.

How many and what kind of military vehicles did Sisera have? (Judges 4:3)

_____

What kind of vehicles?

_____

How many?

_____

The plain of Esdraelon was ideal terrain for armored warfare. Deborah knew that. She also knew that Sisera wanted to meet the Israelites on level ground, not in the mountains. A woman of wisdom, she took advantage of Sisera's passion. She knew she could not lure him into the mountains to fight. She also knew that arrogant Sisera would scorn a woman leader, and would look on Barak, who submitted to a woman's leadership, as a weakling and a coward.

Deborah took full advantage of these facts. As a ju jitsu fighter knows how to use an opponent's weight against him by pulling him off balance, so Deborah used Sisera's judgements against him. She began by setting up an ambush.

How many Israelites had responded to the call to fight Sisera? (Judges 4:10)

_____ 300

_____ 666

_____ 40,000

_____ 10,000

From which tribes did they come? (Judges 4:6, 10)

1. _____

2. _____

Deborah knew that Sisera believed Barak was a coward. She took advantage of that. After her troops had gathered on the plain of Esdraelon, they turned and looked toward Sisera's armored chariots, which had gathered in the foothills ready to do battle on the plain. Then, once they saw the terrifying enemy, she told them to flee, as if they were afraid to fight.

Where did Barak and his troops go? (Judges 4:6, 12)

_____

It looked as if the bulk of her army had deserted, fleeing to Mt. Tabor. Deborah was left with only a small company of soldiers from the tribe of Ephraim. They were gathered on the plain of Esdraelon, through which ran the Kishon River. The Kishon was actually not a river, but a small stream which ran through the center of the great plain, bordered on each side by low, swampy soil. But Deborah had a battle plan.

Deborah knew a great deal about Sisera. She knew, for instance, that Sisera was a chauvinist who disrespected women. We discover this in the victory song Deborah sang after she defeated Sisera. In one of the verses she sings of Sisera's mother, waiting back in the Canaanite city, wondering why her son is so long in returning from the battle. One of the mother's lady friends reminds her that Sisera probably had other things on his mind than coming home to see his mother following the victory.

How did they expect Sisera to treat the women after he won the battle? (Judges 5:30)

Knowing that Sisera was a chauvinist, Deborah played to this weakness. She deliberately put herself at the front of the small army of Ephraimites and taunted Sisera to come fight her on the plain.

Who took the word to Sisera that Barak had fled, leaving Deborah and her small band of soldiers on the plain? (Judges 4:11-12)

The Kenites were not Hebrews, but were Midianites.

From whom had Heber, the Kenite, descended? (Judges 4:11)

Many years before, when Moses and the Israelites were leaving Mt. Sinai making their way north to the Promised Land of Canaan, Moses asked the brother of his Midianite wife, Zipporah, to go before them as a scout, or guide.

What was the name of Moses' brother-in-law? (Numbers 10:29)

What had Moses promised him as a reward? (Numbers 10:32)

The descendants of Hobab were called Kenites.

What evidence do we have that Moses' promise to Hobab was fulfilled? (Judges 1:16, I Samuel 15:6)

_____

_____

Deborah knew that Heber, while still looking like a Midianite, was loyal to the Hebrew people. She let him take the message to Sisera that Barak had fled and that Deborah was left alone on the plain. It was all Sisera needed. He ordered an attack on this old Jewish woman who dared stand on the plain taunting him—having no idea she had set up an ambush to lure him and his heavy chariots into the swamp surrounding the Kishon River.

Who had Deborah told Barak would fight the battle for them? (Judges 4:14)

_____

_____

What happened when Sisera ordered his heavy, iron chariots into the swampy land next to the river? (Judges 4:15)

_____

_____

When the heavy rains came what happened to the chariots? (Judges 5:21)

_____

_____

At that point, a signal was given and Barak and his 20,000 warriors descended from nearby Mt. Tabor. Sisera's men were forced to abandon their chariots, now mired in the mud, and flee on foot.

What became of the troops of Sisera? (Judges 4:16)

_____

_____

What did Sisera do? (Judges 4:17)

_____

_____

Ignorant of the history of the Kenites, and their intense loyalty to the Hebrew people, Sisera fled to the tent of Heber, hoping to find a place where he could hide.

Who came out to meet him? (Judges 4:18)

_____

What was Sisera, the chauvinist, forced to do? (Judges 4:19-20)

_____

_____

_____

What did Jael, the wife of Heber, do after Sisera fell asleep in her tent? (Judges 4:21)

_____

_____

_____

_____

It was a great victory, not only for the Jews, but for women as well. Both Deborah and Jael emerged as national heroes. This was followed by a time of peace.

How long did the peace last? (Judges 5:31)

_____

WRAP UP

God uses whom He chooses. God is not a chauvinist nor a feminist. God makes no distinction between men and women. He is simply looking for someone who is obedient, who is willing to allow the Holy Spirit to use him or her to bring glory to the Father. Deborah didn't set out to be a judge, and certainly not a military leader. She was a good wife, raised her children, and dedicated her natural abilities to God for His service. Deborah is the perfect example of how God uses a person who follows the advice of Solomon in Ecclesiastes 9:10. "Whatever your hand finds to do, do it with all your might. . . ."

FINAL LESSON

Deborah is the first woman in Scripture to prove what Paul told the early church was God's intent for the Kingdom of God. "There is neither Jew nor Greek, slave nor free, male nor female, for you are all one in Christ Jesus" (Galatians 3:28).

PERSONAL REVIEW QUESTIONS

Circle T (true) or F (false)

1. T   F   God prefers to use men to lead.

2. T   F   Deborah was God's second choice since He couldn't find a man to do the job.

3. T   F   God used Deborah because she was the best qualified person and because she was willing to be used.

4. T   F   God let Deborah prove herself for many years before He used her as a national hero.

5. T   F   Deborah was already respected as a woman of wisdom before the battle with Sisera.

6. T   F   Deborah knew she could not match Sisera's physical strength, so she used other gifts to defeat him.

7. T   F   Barak respected the fact God had selected Deborah.

8. T   F   Both Barak and Heber were willing to follow Deborah's leadership, even though in that day men had little respect for women.

9. T   F   Deborah could not have defeated Sisera had the Lord not intervened with a flash flood.

10. T   F   God does not judge people by their sex.

MEMORY VERSE

Proverbs 31:30 (Memorize, then write it on these lines.)

_____

_____

_____

_____

TRUE OR FALSE ANSWERS:

1-F, 2-F, 3-T, 4-T, 5-T, 6-T, 7-T, 8-T, 9-T, 10-T

NOTES

Lesson 4
Gideon
God's Plan Works Best

SCRIPTURE: Judges 6-8
VIDEO REFERENCE: Lesson #4
SUPPLEMENTARY READING REFERENCE:
Ten Bible People Like Me
Chapter IV: "Gideon: The Courageous Coward"

1. Introduction

Following the death of Deborah, the nation of Israel, without a strong leader, once again drifted back into the worship of heathen gods. When this happened, the anointing of God departed, and for seven years the people were on their own.

Why did God withdraw his protection from Israel? (Judges 6:1)

_____

Which false gods were the Israelites serving? (Judges 6:10)

_____

When God's protection was withdrawn from the nation, who rushed in to take over? (Judges 6:1)

_____

The Midianites were tribes of desert nomads who haunted the eastern borderlands. They occasionally joined forces with a group of bandits called Amalekites who raided the nation of Israel at will.

What were the tactics of the Midianites and Amalekites? (Judges 6:3-4)

_____

The Israelites, weakened by their worship of false gods, were no match for the desert marauders. Israel was still a new nation, still divided into tribal areas. The Midianite raids created a terrifying hardship for the Israelites, who were struggling to eke out an existence from the stony soil of this land they had so recently occupied. All of their time needed to be consumed trying to make a living. There was no time, nor did the people have any heart, to engage in constant warfare. They were desperate.

What did the Israelites do in their desperation? (Judges 6:6)

_____

After the Israelites began to call on God for help, God sent a nameless prophet into their midst to (1) remind them of something, and (2) to warn them of something.

What did the prophet remind them of? (Judges 6:7-9)

_____

_____

_____

What warning did the prophet bring? (Judges 6:10)

_____

_____

2. The Call of God

Like most Israelites, Gideon was a simple farmer. He lived near his father in the little village near where Deborah had held court.

What was the name of Gideon's village? (Judges 6:11)

_____ Ophrah

_____ Joash

_____ Abiezrite

What was Gideon's father's name? (Judges 6:11)

_____ Ophrah

_____ Joash

_____ Abiezrite

What was Gideon doing when the angel of the Lord called him? (Judges 6:11)

_____

Normally wheat was threshed on a big, flat rock in an exposed place. Here, as the farmer flailed the wheat, the wind would blow away the chaff, or husks, leaving the wheat grain on the rock. Gideon, however, afraid of the Midianites, was threshing wheat down in a winepress. To all outward appearances Gideon was a coward, like the rest of the Israelites. God, however, who does not look on the outward appearance, saw something else in Gideon.

What did the angel call Gideon? (Judges 6:12)

_____

How did Gideon respond to the angel? (Judges 6:13)

_____

_____

_____

Although Gideon is listed among the heroes of faith in Hebrews 11:32, we see he was not a bold, dashing leader. It's not that he was a coward. Rather, he was cautious and inhibited. This shows it is not just triumphant faith that God rewards. He rewards small faith as well.

How much faith did Jesus say was necessary to do big things? (Matthew 17:20)

_____

Gideon was a harassed and discouraged man. He bore the burdens of long defeat. He had no one to stand with him and no traditions to fall back on. He had no concept of the law of Moses, meaning he knew virtually nothing about the Bible of the day. When the angel called him, he responded with bitter skepticism and lack of understanding. He was a very unlikely man to call to lead the nation. Yet God saw something in him that Gideon didn't even see in himself.

How much personal strength did the angel say was necessary to save Israel from the Midianites? (Judges 6:14)

_____

Why was this all the strength Gideon needed? (Judges 6:14, 16)

_____

Gideon was not a coward, but he was cautious. He asked the angel for three separate signs that God was calling him.

What were the three signs? (Judges 6:17)

1. (Judges 6:20-21) _____

_____

_____

_____

2. (Judges 6:36-38) _____

_____

_____

_____

3. (Judges 6:39-40) _____

_____

_____

_____

The Bible has many stories of God calling men out of the world to serve Him in a special way.

List those God called to serve Him.

1. (Hebrews 11:8) _____

2. (Exodus 3:2-4) _____

3. (Deuteronomy 31:23) _____

4. (I Samuel 3:4) _____

5. (I Samuel 16:1-13) _____

6. (II Kings 9:6) _____

7. (Isaiah 6:1-9) _____

8. (Amos 7:14-15) _____

9. (Matthew 4:18-19) _____

10. (" " " ") _____

11. (Matthew 4:21-22) _____

12. (" " " ") _____

13. (Mark 2:14) _____

14. (Mark 10:17-22) _____

15. (Acts 13:2) _____

16. (" " ") _____

17. (I Thessalonians 2:11-12) _____

3. Courage Wins over Fear

Gideon knew that he had to do more than see signs. He had to act on his faith. Especially was this necessary in Gideon's case, since he was a fearful man and it required great courage—as well as great faith—to obey.

What difficult thing did God ask Gideon to do? (Judges 6:25-26)

_____

_____

_____

The god Baal took many forms in the Old Testament. The early Baals were related to a specific deity, Hadad, the Semitic storm-god and the most important god in Canaan. Some sources say Baal was the son of Dagon, the principal deity the Philistines worshipped in Samson's time in Gaza. The Baals were also related, in some unknown way, to a female goddess called Asherah. During the days of Elijah, the evil queen, Jezebel, wife of King Ahab, brought with her from Phoenicia almost 1000 priests and prophets of both Asherah and a fearsome Baal called Melqart who demanded human sacrifice. On several occasions Baal is connected with a horrible god of the Ammonites named Molech to whom children were burned as sacrifices.

While the Jews were strictly forbidden by God to worship any god but Jehovah, the Canaanites—who still lived in the land now occupied by the Israelites—worshiped many false gods. Throughout the land of Canaan there could be found alters to Baal. Often a grove of trees would be dedicated as a sacred place of worship to a false god. The Canaanites erected poles, similar to totum poles, to worship Asherah. Without strong spiritual leadership it was easy for the Israelites to begin to combine their worship of Jehovah with the worship of false gods.

God had specifically commanded the Israelites to deal with these false gods.

How were they to keep free from the false gods? (Judges 2:2)

1. _____

2. _____

Following the death of Joshua, what did the Israelites do? (Judges 2:11-13)

_____

_____

_____

As long as the people had the strong leadership of a judge, for the most part they worshiped Jehovah.

What happened after each judge died, however? (Judges 2:19)

_____

_____

_____

To whom did the Baal altar and the Asherah pole in the town of Ophrah belong? (Judges 6:25)

_____

Why did Gideon tear down the altar to Baal at night? (Judges 6:27)

_____

_____

When Joash, Gideon's father, saw the decisiveness of his son—a son who had always been fearful and indecisive—he realized God must have called him to special ministry. Thus when the people of the town, furious that Gideon had ripped down the altar, demanded that Joash present him to the mob so they could kill him, Joash moved to his defense. Perhaps Joash had known, for a long time, that he should have torn down the altar himself. But he, too, had been indecisive. Now the deed was done and Joash saw the rightness of it.

What did Joash tell the townspeople? (Judges 6:31)

_____

_____

_____

What was the meaning of the new name Joash gave his son? (Judges 6:32)

_____

Throughout this story we see God transforming a cowardly man into a man of courage. The first time we meet Gideon he is hiding from the Midianites. Now we discover he was also afraid of his family and the Israelites in Ophrah. Gradually, though, he is changing. Even though he is afraid of the people, his faith is greater than his fear. He obeys God and rips down the false altars.

Now an even greater danger faces him.

What was the greater danger facing Gideon and the people of Israel? (Judges 6:33)

_____

_____

What happened to Gideon that gave this former coward additional courage? (Judges 6:34)

_____

Gideon then sent out a call for recruits—calling them to arms. A total of 32,000 men responded. It was at that time Gideon asked for the two additional signs from God. These involved the lamb's fleeces he laid on the ground. Gideon's yearning for a "sign" from God was part of his fearful, cautious nature. God was giving him courage, but he wanted to be certain he was following God—not self. Even though he had an army of 32,000, it was far smaller than the amassed armies of the Midianites and Amalekites.

How large was the army of the enemy? (Judges 6:5, 7:12)

_____

By actual count after the battle, how many enemy soldiers were there? (Judges 8:10)

_____

God honored Gideon's desire to do things "God's way" and gave him the signs he asked for. God then tested Gideon by telling him his army of 32,000 was too large to fight the enemy army several times that size.

Why did God want Gideon to fight the enemy with an even smaller army? (Joshua 7:2)

_____

How did Gideon slim down his army? (Judges 7:3)

_____

After the cowards departed how many did he have left? (Judges 7:3)

_____ 32,000

_____ 22,000

_____ 10,000

_____ 300

Now came a further test. Gideon was camped on the slopes of the hills. The men were desperate with thirst, but the springs lay at the foot where the riders of the raiding tribes could sweep down on them. The test was devised to separate those whose thirst made them forget about the enemy from those who knew it was imperative to remain alert at all times. Those who remained alert did not kneel to drink, but picked the water up with their hands.

How many knelt and slurped the water? (Judges 7:6)

_____ 22,000

_____ 10,000

_____ 9,700

_____ 300

How many picked up the water and lapped it out of their hands? (Judges 7:6)

_____ 10,000

_____ 9,700

_____ 300

God realizes Gideon is still fearful—and this time with good reason. He only has 300 men. That means he cannot fight the enemy by conventional means. This time, instead of waiting for Gideon to ask for another sign, God gives him one. But to receive the sign Gideon is required to do something courageous.

What did God tell Gideon he would have to do? (Judges 7:9-11)

_____

_____

What was the name of Gideon's servant who went with him? (Judges 7:10)

_____

Add him to the list of faithful servants in the Bible who were willing to follow their leaders regardless of the cost. Some are well known—Joshua followed Moses, Zadok followed David, Jonathan had his armorbearer, Elisha followed Elijah, Timothy followed Paul. Thank God for faithful followers.

4. God's Minority

What was the dream Gideon overheard while he was on his spy mission? (Judges 7:13)

_____

_____

_____

Barley was a common, poorer crop, grown on less productive ground in the hill country. Camped on the Jezreel Plain, the Midianites were out of their proper element. They knew they belonged in the hills.

How did the Midianite soldier interpret his friend's dream? (Judges 7:14)

_____

_____

What was Gideon's first reaction on overhearing the dream interpreted? (Judges 7:15)

_____

Then what did he do? (Judges 7:15-16)

_____

_____

_____

What happened when Gideon's 300 did what he told them to do? (Judges 7:22)

_____

_____

_____

When the enemy fled back toward the Jordan Valley, Gideon sent word to the leaders of the tribe of Ephraim. The soldiers of Ephraim met the enemy as they tried to ford the Jordan River and finished them off. Then the leaders of Ephraim criticized Gideon for not asking them to help him in the initial battle.

How did Gideon answer the leaders of Ephraim? (Judges 8:2-3)

_____ He told them it was none of their business.

_____ He told them if they complained he'd wipe them out, too.

_____ He challenged them to fight him at Oreb and Zeeb.

_____ He gave them credit for the victory, saying what they did was far greater than what he did.

Gideon and his 300 men then pursued the remnant of the army, now only 15,000, and caught up with them east of Jordan.

What was the result of that battle? (Judges 8:11-12)

_____

Following this, Gideon returned through the tribal areas, punishing all the elders who had refused to help him.

How did the Israelites want to reward Gideon? (Judges 8:22)

_____

What was Gideon's answer? (Judges 8:23)

_____

Following Gideon's death what did the Israelites do? (Judges 8:33-35)

1. _____
2. _____
3. _____
4. _____

WRAP UP

The story of Gideon shows that God, who looks on the heart, is able to take a man who seems to be a coward and turn him into a hero—as long as that man is willing to do things God's way.

FINAL LESSON

One man, with God, is a majority.

PERSONAL REVIEW QUESTIONS

Circle T (true) or F (false)

1. T   F   Gideon was threshing wheat in the winepress to keep his father from sacrificing the grain to Baal.

2. T   F   The angel of the Lord made fun of Gideon for being in the winepress.

3.   T   F   Gideon was too drunk on wine to answer the angel.

4.   T   F   Gideon immediately volunteered to save Israel.

5.   T   F   Gideon had about as much faith as a grain of mustard seed—but God used that for good.

6.   T   F   Gideon tested God by putting fleeces on the ground.

7.   T   F   Gideon's father was a Baal worshipper.

8.   T   F   God wanted Gideon to fight the Midianites with a small army so God would get the credit if they won.

9.   T   F   Gideon chose the men for his final army by seeing how they drank water from the spring.

10.   T   F   Gideon's army numbered only 300 when he went into battle.

11.   T   F   When Gideon's army waved their torches and blew their trumpets, the enemy soldiers began to kill each other.

12.   T   F   The Israelites wanted to make Gideon king, but he wisely recommended his son, Abimelech, instead.

MEMORY VERSE

Matthew 17:20 (Memorize, then write it on these lines.)

_____

_____

_____

_____

TRUE OR FALSE ANSWERS:

1-F, 2-F, 3-F, 4-F, 5-F, 6-T, 7-T, 8-T, 9-T, 10-T, 11-T, 12-F

NOTES

Lesson 5
David
Learning From Your Mistakes

SCRIPTURE: I Chronicles 13-15
(Also: I Samuel 4:1-7:2, II Samuel 5:17-6:23)
VIDEO REFERENCE: Lesson #5
SUPPLEMENTARY READING REFERENCE:
Ten Bible People Like Me
Chapter V: "David: Learning From Your Mistakes"

1. A Man After God's Own Heart

When Saul was king of Israel he turned away from God, disobeying him on a number of occasions. Finally the prophet Samuel confronted him, telling him his time was short and that God had appointed another to succeed him because he had not obeyed the Lord's commands.

What kind of man did Samuel say God had chosen to succeed Saul?
(I Samuel 13:14)

_____

_____

Almost a thousand years later the Apostle Paul, preaching in Pisidian Antioch, described David in similar terms.

What kind of man did Paul say David was? (Acts 13:22)

_____

_____

_____

This is a strange description, for an outward look at David indicates he did many things that were "ungodly."

1. Fleeing from King Saul, David became a liar. **To whom did he lie?** (I Samuel 21:1-2)

_____

2. Caught in his lies, David was forced to become a deceiver. **How did David deceive the king of Gath?** (I Samuel 21:12-13)

_____

_____

3. He became a traitor and fought against his own people while living with the enemies of the Israelites. **With whom did David join forces?** (I Samuel 27:7)

_____

4. He was a poor judge of people, and did not get rid of the corrupt and ambitious leaders in his army. **What was the name of the murderous soldier David did not punish?** (II Samuel 3:26-27)

_____

5. He was an adulterer. **With whom did David commit adultery?** (II Samuel 11:2-5)

_____

6. He was a murderer. **What was the name of the loyal soldier David had killed to cover up his adultery?** (II Samuel 11:14-17)

_____

7. His home was not in order. **What was the name of David's son who raped his sister?** (II Samuel 13:1, 14)

_____

8. **What was the name of David's son who killed his brother and later tried to kill David?** (II Samuel 13:28, 15:14)

_____

Despite all this, God said,"I have found David, son of Jesse, a man after my own heart; he will do everything I want him to" (Acts 13:22).

2. The Ark of the Covenant

The Ark of the Covenant was a rectangular box made of acacia wood. It had been built by Moses after the Israelites left Egypt and gathered at Mt. Sinai to receive the law. It was four and a half feet long by two and a half feet wide. It was covered with gold and was carried on poles inserted in rings at the four lower corners. The lid, or "mercy seat," was solid gold plate adorned with two golden cherubs with outspread wings. Inside were the two stone tablets Moses had brought down from Mt. Sinai with the Ten Commandments written on them, a pot of manna from the wilderness, and Aaron's rod which had budded. It was the symbol of the divine presence of God.

Every time the Israelites moved from one place to another the Ark went before them, carried by four Levites. When Joshua led the Israelites across the Jordan River into the Promised Land, the Ark went before them. When the Israelites marched around the city of Jericho seven times, they followed the Ark. Later it was enshrined in the tabernacle at Shiloh until the time of Eli, the high priest. Every time the Israelites went into battle during the reign of King Saul, they took the Ark with them. Indeed, as long as the divine presence of God was with them, they were invincible.

But the people became corrupt. They began using the Ark as a good luck charm—depending on it rather than on the living God it represented.

God, however, wanted the people to depend on Him, not the Ark. Therefore, He allowed the Ark to be captured.

What enemy force captured the Ark from the Israelites? (I Samuel 4:10-11)

_____

The two corrupt sons of the high priest, Eli, were killed in battle that day.

What were the names of the sons of Eli? (I Samuel 4:11)

1. _____

2. _____

What happened to Eli when a messenger brought word of the defeat? (I Samuel 4:17-18)

_____

_____

What happened to Eli's daughter-in-law, the wife of his dead son Phinehas, when she heard the news? (I Samuel 4:19-20)

_____

_____

_____

What did the dying wife of Phinehas call her newborn son? (I Samuel 4:21)

_____

What does the name mean? (I Samuel 4:22)

_____

_____

What did the Philistines do with the captured Ark? (I Samuel 5:1-2)

_____

_____

What happened to the Philistine god, Dagon, when they left the Ark in the heathen temple? (I Samuel 5:3-5)

_____

_____

_____

_____

The Philistines suffered greatly after they acquired the Ark of the Covenant. Their land was overrun with rats which carried the deadly black plague. The people, swelling with tumors in the groin—which accompanies the plague—died by the scores. The Philistine leaders sent the Ark from Ashdod to Gath. But the plague followed, and the entire city was afflicted. The Ark was transferred to another Philistine city, Ekron, where an even worse plague took place.

How long did the Philistines keep the Ark? (I Samuel 6:1)

_____ Seven years

_____ Forty years

_____ Seven months

Desperate for help, the Philistine leaders finally put the Ark on a cart pulled by two cows. They sent the cart across the border and the cows brought it into a little Israelite village.

What was the name of the village where the Ark was returned? (I Samuel 6:13-14)

_____

The Levites in Beth Shemesh recognized the Ark of the Covenant. They removed it from the cart and the people sacrificed to God, celebrating its return. Then tragedy happened.

Why did 70 men in Beth Shemesh (some ancient Bible manuscripts say the number was 50,070 men) die? (I Samuel 6:19)

_____

_____

Where did the Israelites finally store the Ark? (I Samuel 7:1)

_____

While the Ark was in the house of Abinadab, in a tiny village less than seven miles from Jerusalem, the prophet Samuel called the people to repentance.

What did Samuel tell the people they had to do to get the Philistines off their back? (I Samuel 7:3)

_____

_____

_____

How did the people respond? (I Samuel 7:4)

_____

_____

How long did the Ark remain in the house of Abinadab? (I Samuel 7:2)

_____ Seven months

_____ Seven years

_____ Forty years

_____ Twenty years

3. David and the Ark

While the Ark was resting in the house of Abinadab, David was named King of Judah—the southern portion of the land of Israel. He established Jerusalem as the capital of the nation. In an effort to unite the entire nation under his leadership, he called together the military, political, and religious leaders and made a suggestion.

What did David want to do? (I Chronicles 13:3)

_____

How did the people respond to this suggestion? (I Chronicles 13:4)

_____

David chose the same method used by the Philistines to move the Ark.

How did David move the Ark from the house of Abinidab? (II Samuel 6:3-4)

_____

_____

What were the names of the two sons of Abinidab who were accompanying the cart with the Ark? (II Samuel 6:3)

1. _____
2. _____

What were David and the Israelites doing as the procession started toward Jerusalem? (II Samuel 6:5)

_____

_____

They had only gone a short way when the oxen pulling the cart stumbled and one of the men reached out to steady the Ark.

Who put his hand on the Ark? (II Samuel 6:6)

_____

What happened to him when he touched the Ark? (II Samuel 6:7)

_____

Afraid to continue, David stopped the procession and put the Ark in the home of a local man.

Where did David store the Ark? (II Samuel 6:10)

_____

How long was the Ark there? (II Samuel 6:11)

_____ Seven years

_____ Seven months

_____ Three years

_____ Three months

David realized he had made a mistake. Instead of trying to bluff his way through, he returned to Jerusalem to pray and study the law of Moses.

What did David discover about the Ark? (I Chronicles 15:2)

_____

_____

What had David learned in the Scriptures about carrying the Ark? (I Chronicles 15:15)

_____

_____

What did David say he should have done before picking up the Ark? (I Chronicles 15:13b)

_____

_____

Who did the singing and celebrating the first time David tried to move the Ark? (I Chronicles 13:8)

_____

The second time the Israelites moved the Ark, they did it with great precision. Earlier, David had used organization rather than depending on the Holy Spirit to interpret to him the Word of God. Now he discovered that while God is a God of enthusiasm, he does not bless impetuousness. David had learned by his mistakes.

Who did the singing and celebrating the second time they moved the Ark? (I Chronicles 15:16)

_____

_____

What process was used to bring the Ark from the house of Obed-Edom to Jerusalem? (II Samuel 6:15)

_____

57

What was David doing as the Ark was being moved on the shoulders of the Levites? (II Samuel 6:14-15)

_____

_____

After making a horrible mistake, David corrected it by doing six things:

(1) He went back and studied his Bible (when all else fails, read the manual).

(2) He sought counsel from wise men.

(3) He determined to follow God's plan, no matter how foolish or unpopular it seemed.

(4) He communicated with his people.

(5) He organized his men and put the men he felt God had chosen in leadership.

(6) Only then did he move ahead.

David had prepared a new tabernacle in Jerusalem on Mt. Zion. Here the Ark would remain until it was placed in Solomon's temple following David's death.

What was the Tabernacle of David? (I Chronicles 16:1)

_____

The Tabernacle of David was different from the Tabernacle of Moses which came before, and from the temple which followed. It did not have an outer court or a "Holy of Holies." It was a simple, open tent and people could come and go at all times, freely worshipping God, singing and dancing before him. During this time many of the Psalms were composed. "From Zion, perfect in beauty, God shines forth" (Psalm 50:2).

The Tabernacle of David lasted only one generation. Then the presence of God was once more confined to a temple.

Many years later the prophet Amos prophesied that a day would come, sometime in the future, when God would "restore David's fallen tent." God said in that day He would "repair its broken places, restore its ruins, and build it as it used to be." This was later confirmed in the book of Acts when James spoke to the Council of Elders meeting in Jerusalem. James said that when the Gentiles received the Holy Spirit, it was the fulfillment of Amos' prophecy that the Tabernacle of David was once again being restored.

Most Bible scholars believe David composed and was singing Psalm 24 as he danced before the Ark. He knew, because he had learned from his mistakes, that God had forgiven him—that he was, indeed, a man after God's own heart.

Who did David say could ascend Mt. Zion (the hill of the Lord)? (Psalm 24:3-4)

_____

_____

_____

WRAP UP

David was a man after God's own heart because he was teachable and humble. After each mistake we find him repenting and—equally important—learning.

FINAL LESSON

God loves to use men who have botched up their lives, repented, and learned from their mistakes.

PERSONAL REVIEW QUESTIONS

Circle T (true) or F (false)

1. T   F   Despite his mistakes, David is listed as one of the finest leaders in history.

2. T   F   David never made any major mistakes, only little ones.

3. T   F   David learned from his mistakes.

4. T   F   God can use men and women who make mistakes as long as they are teachable.

5. T   F   Simon Peter called David a man after God's own heart.

6. T   F   The Ark represented God's holy presence.

7. T   F   Ichabod means God is in control.

8. T   F   Ichabod means the glory of God has departed.

9. T   F   God demands reverence except from those who don't know who He is.

10. T   F   God blessed David when he tried to do things God's way.

MEMORY VERSE

Psalm 24:3-4 (Memorize, then write it on these lines.)

_____

_____

_____

_____

TRUE OR FALSE ANSWERS:

1-T, 2-F, 3-T, 4-T, 5-F, 6-T, 7-F, 8-T, 9-F, 10-T

NOTES

Lesson 6
Elijah
Always Enough

SCRIPTURE: I Kings 17—19
VIDEO REFERENCE: Lesson #6
SUPPLEMENTARY READING REFERENCE:
  Ten Bible People Like Me
  Chapter VI: "Elijah: Always Enough"

1. Definition of Prosperity

God's people, the Bible says, shall prosper. In fact, prosperity is one of the major themes of the Bible.

But prosperity does not necessarily mean wealth and riches. It simply means that when God calls a person, He also provides to that person ample supplies to get the job done.

Prosperity then means: Having enough to achieve what God calls you to do.

2. Bible Promises and Examples

While the King James Version of the Bible uses the word "success" only once—when God promises Joshua "success" if he obeys God (Joshua 1:8)—the word "prosper" appears many times. In other translations of the Bible, "prosper" or "prosperity" is often translated "success" or "succeed."

The first time the promise of prosperity is found in the Bible is when Abraham told his servant, as he sent him to find a wife for his son, Isaac, that God would prosper him.

How was God going to prosper the servant? (Genesis 24:40)

_____

_____

_____

This was a promise for a specific kind of prosperity. There are other Bible promises for overall prosperity. All these promises, except one, are found in the Old Testament. Most of them have to do with material prosperity.

In David's charge to his son, Solomon, he said that if Solomon would obey God by following His inner voice and keeping the written law, God would prosper him.

In what ways would God prosper Solomon if he obeyed? (I Kings 2:3)

The one New Testament reference to prosperity does not have to do with material prosperity, although it is combined with John's prayer that his friend, Gaius, have good health.

What part of Gaius has prospered? (III John 2)

In Genesis 39 we find additional insight as to how God prospers people. This is the story of Joseph, the son of Jacob, who had been sold into Egyptian slavery by his jealous brothers. He was bought by an Egyptian army officer and put in charge of the household. Although God did not deliver him from slavery, the Bible says God "prospered" him (Genesis 39:2-3). Later, Joseph was thrown into prison on a trumped-up charge.

Although God did not set Joseph free from prison, what did God do for him in prison? (Genesis 39:23)

For every promise of prosperity found in the Bible, there are twice as many warnings that prosperity can destroy a person. As a rule of thumb we can say: Bible "prosperity" is usually given at a specific point of need so the person can do what God has called him to do, and is always given for the glory of God.

By that definition, Elijah was a prosperous man. Yet he had nothing of this world's goods. In fact, most of his life was spent clashing with the rich and the famous. By the world's standards he was poor. He never owned a home. He didn't even have transportation, walking (or running) everywhere he went. On several occasions he ran out of food completely, and his life was constantly threatened by those he opposed. Yet he was a "prosperous" man in that he always had enough to do what God called him to do— as well as enough to share with others.

3. **Elijah the Man**

Elijah was born around 900 B.C. in the small village of Tishbe east of the Jordan River in northern Israel. It was a rugged, mountainous area with long, dry summers and temperatures that often exceeded 100 degrees.

Bad times began shortly after Elijah, about 30 years old, left home and, on command of God, confronted Ahab, the wicked king of northern Israel.

Ahab was using slave labor to build an opulent palace in the city of Samaria. His wife, Jezebel, was a fanatical worshipper of Baal. She was enticing many of the Jewish priests to become Baal worshippers. Elijah, wearing only a leather loin cloth, sandals, and a hairy animal hide cloak (called a mantle), marched into Ahab's palace.

What did Elijah tell Ahab? (I Kings 17:1)

_____

_____

Furious, Ahab called for Elijah's arrest. But the young prophet took off running until he came to a deep canyon, or wadi, where he hid.

How did God feed Elijah? (I Kings 17:6)

_____

_____

_____

Why did the brook dry up? (I Kings 17:7)

_____

Elijah was learning that when God withholds the rain to punish the unjust, the just suffer also. However, just because the water had run out was not to say God was not prospering him.

Where did God tell Elijah to go so he could have food and drink? (I Kings 17:9)

_____

Elijah did not complain about his exile in the wilderness, nor did he complain about the lack of food and water. Instead, he believed that as long as he obeyed God, God would take care of him. So, leaving the wilderness, he headed north for the Lebanese coast and the village of Zarephath.

Who was the first person Elijah saw on entering the town? (I Kings 17:10)

_____

_____

What did he ask for? (I Kings 17:10-11)

_____

_____

What was her response? (I Kings 17:12)

_____

_____

_____

What strange, seemingly selfish, request did Elijah make? (I Kings 17:13)

_____

_____

_____

What did Elijah promise the widow if she fed him out of her meager supplies? (I Kings 17:14)

_____ That God would send ravens to feed her.

_____ That God would send rain and her fields would produce crops.

_____ That King Ahab would send food.

_____ That the flour and oil would be supernaturally replenished every day until it rained in the land.

_____ That God would answer her prayers and give her a rich husband.

How much food was provided every day? (I Kings 17:15)

_____ Enough for the widow.

_____ Enough for the widow and her family.

_____ Enough for the widow, her family, and Elijah.

How did the widow show her appreciation to Elijah? (I Kings 17:19)

_____

_____

What miracle did Elijah perform so the woman would know she had blessed a man of God? (I Kings 17:17-24)

_____

_____

_____

_____

4. Principles of Prosperity

Who is the source of our prosperity (success)? (Nehemiah 2:20)

_____

What happens when we disobey God's commands? (II Chronicles 24:20)

_____

_____

What happens when we forsake the Lord? (II Chronicles 24:20)

_____ He destroys us.

_____ He causes us to be sick.

_____ He makes our children sick.

_____ He forgives us and says it's okay.

_____ He forsakes us, meaning we become our own source for success and prosperity, rather than God's being our source.

Can you expect to prosper if you sin and then try to cover it up? (Proverbs 28:13)

_____ Yes, because God does not want us to let other people know about our sins and weaknesses.

_____ No. God blesses and prospers those who confess and renounce their sin.

Whom does God richly bless? (Proverbs 28:20)

_____

What happens if we seek material prosperity and riches? (Proverbs 28:20)

_____

What are we to seek rather than material prosperity and riches? (Matthew 6:33)

_____

If we seek first God's Kingdom and His righteousness, what will God do? (Matthew 6:33)

_____

_____

Whom will God prosper? (Proverbs 28:25b)

_____

How can we guarantee we'll lack nothing? (Proverbs 28:27)

_____

WRAP UP

1. God provides in special ways for those who obey Him.

2. God wants us to share, even out of our need, with those who have greater needs.

3. When we give to others out of our need, God gives to us out of His abundance.

FINAL LESSON

God always provides enough for us to do what He has asked us to do. If provision is not there, it is because:

1. We are trying to do something God has not asked us to do;

2. Our timing is bad;

3. We are trying to do more than God has asked us to do; or,

4. We are disobeying God in some other area of our lives.

PERSONAL REVIEW QUESTIONS

Circle T (true) or F (false)

1. T F God wants all his children to drive Cadillacs.

2. T F All we have to do to prosper is obey God.

3. T F God promises to bless those who give to the poor.

4. T F God's idea of prosperity may be different from our idea.

5. T F Elijah complained about the lack of food until God sent ravens to feed him.

6. T F Elijah said it was not fair that the water in his stream dried up.

7.   T   F   When Elijah delivered God's warning to Ahab, the king immediately repented.

8.   T   F   The widow of Zarepath refused to help Elijah until he convinced her he was a prophet.

9.   T   F   The widow of Zarepath acted in faith and shared her final food with Elijah.

10. T   F   God blessed the widow of Zarepath by letting her win the state lottery.

11. T   F   Prosperity means having enough to do what God has called you to do.

12. T   F   God wants all His children to prosper.

MEMORY VERSE

Psalm 37:25 (Memorize, then write it on these lines)

_____

_____

_____

_____

TRUE OR FALSE ANSWERS:

1-F, 2-T, 3-T, 4-T, 5-F, 6-F, 7-F, 8-F, 9-T, 10-F, 11-T, 12-T

NOTES

Lesson 7
John the Baptist
A Man of Integrity

SCRIPTURE: Matthew 3:1-17
VIDEO REFERENCE: Lesson #7
SUPPLEMENTARY READING REFERENCE:
    Ten Bible People Like Me
    Chapter VII: "John the Baptist: A Man of Integrity"

1. Beginnings

After the death of the prophet Malachi, the Jews went for almost 400 years without hearing the prophetic voice of God. No one was speaking for God. Then a man named John appeared on the scene. He was the last of the Old Testament prophets, and the one who introduced the New Testament.

John was born six months before Jesus in the tiny village of Ein Karem just outside Jerusalem. His mother, Elizabeth, was closely related to Mary, the mother of Jesus. Some even think they might have been sisters.

While Jesus was raised in Nazareth and went to work in Joseph's carpenter's shop, early in life John left Ein Karem—perhaps at the death of his parents—and joined a group known as the Essenes in the Negev desert.

The Essenes majored on goodness. They lived in community, held all property in common, practiced celibacy, and purified themselves repeatedly for the coming Messiah by daily water baptisms.

Believing that God was calling him to prepare the way for the coming Messiah, John left the Essenes and lived alone in the desert. He journeyed into the populated areas to preach, calling on the people to return to God and get ready for the Christ.

2. The Message

What was John's message? (Matthew 3:2)

_____

_____

At the birth of John, his father, Zechariah, had sung a prophetic song.

What did Zechariah say his son would be called? (Luke 1:76)

_____

What did he say his mission would be? (Luke 1:76)

_____

John's purpose was to prepare the way for Jesus. This was done by calling the people to repentance.
How did the people respond when John asked them to repent? (Matthew 3:6)

1. _____

2. _____

3. Repentance

The prophets of the Old Testament had all called the people to repent.

What did Isaiah tell the people to do? (Isaiah 55:7)

_____

_____

_____

What did Isaiah say God would do if the people repented? (Isaiah 55:7)

_____

What did Jeremiah tell the people to do? (Jeremiah 3:12)

_____

What did Jeremiah say God would do if the people repented? (Jeremiah 3:12)

_____

_____

In the days of Ezekiel, the prophet, the people had turned their backs on God's law.

What did God say the Israelites had done instead of keeping His law? (Ezekiel 11:12)

_____

_____

What did Ezekiel tell the people to do? (Ezekiel 14:6)

_____

_____

What did Ezekiel say God would do if the people repented? (Ezekiel 14:11)

_____

_____

_____

What did Hosea tell the people to do? (Hosea 14:1)

_____

_____

What did Joel tell the people to do to show they were repenting? (Joel 2: 12-13)

_____

_____

_____

_____

What did Zechariah say God would do if the people turned to Him? (Zechariah 1:3)

_____

What did Malachi say God would do if the people returned to Him? (Malachi 3:7)

_____

4. Water Baptism

The name "John the Baptist" is not a Biblical name. He was simply called John. However, when he called people to repent, he told them they should be baptized as a sign of that repentance. As a member of the Essene community at Qumran in the Negev Desert, John had probably practiced daily baptism as a purification rite, getting ready for the coming Messiah. Although he had left the Essenes by the time he began his public ministry, water baptism was still at the heart of his call to repentance.

The Greek word, *baptizo*—from which we get our word "baptism"—simply means to immerse, or plunge under. With John, water baptism was the sign that the people had been cleansed of their sin by repenting, and were ready for the Messiah to appear.

Later the Apostle Paul gave new meaning to water baptism by saying it was more than a symbol—that something actually happened in the spirit world when a person submitted to baptism.

What did Paul say happens when we are baptized "into Christ Jesus?" (Romans 6:3)

_____

How are we "buried with Christ?" (Romans 6:4)

_____

What are we baptized into? (Romans 6:4)

_____

As Christ was raised from the dead, what happens to us when we emerge from the baptismal water? (Romans 6:4)

_____

What happens to the "old self" when we are baptized in the name of Jesus? (Romans 6:6)

_____

_____

Paul says water baptism is a spiritual crucifixion where the old man is put to death.

What happens to those who have "died"? (Romans 6:7)

_____

Peter says the water of baptism, while not removing dirt from our bodies, brings something else far greater.

What pledge does water baptism bring with it? (I Peter 3:21)

_____

What did Jesus say about baptism? (Matthew 28:19)

_____

There was a widespread rumor that Jesus also baptized, in fact, that he had baptized more people than John.

Did Jesus actually baptize anyone? (John 4:1-2)

_____ Yes, he baptized more disciples than John.

_____ No, Jesus did not baptize, but his disciples did.

What did Peter say people should do to be saved? (Acts 2:38)

1. _____

2. _____

While John baptized in the name of "repentance," in what name did Peter say people should be baptized? (Acts 2:38)

_____

What did Peter say we would receive if we repented and were baptized in the name of Jesus? (Acts 2:38)

_____ A baptismal certificate.

_____ Membership in a local church.

_____ A beautiful new Bible.

_____ An engraved fountain pen.

_____ The gift of the Holy Spirit.

What did the people of Samaria do after they received Jesus Christ under Philip's preaching? (Acts 8:12)

_____

Philip had a number of famous converts. One of them was Simon, a former expert in voodoo and white magic.

What happened to Simon after he believed? (Acts 8:13)

_____

Another of Philip's converts was an Ethopian eunuch.

What did the eunuch request after he received Jesus as his Lord? (Acts 8:36-38)

_____

Three days after Saul's conversion (his name was later changed to Paul), a man named Ananias came to see him in Damascus. On the road from Jerusalem to Damascus, Saul had had an experience with the risen Christ, Who had appeared to him in a light so bright he had been blinded.

Why did Ananias come to see Saul? (Acts 9:17)

1. _____

2. _____

After this happened to Saul, what did he do? (Acts 9:18-19)
(Check right answers.)

_____ He regained his sight.

_____ He regained his strength.

_____ He regained his appetite.

_____ He was baptized.

What did Paul do to the Philippian jailer and his family after the jailer received Christ? (Acts 16:33)

_____

When Paul came to Ephesus he found a group of believers. They had been baptized either by John, or by one of John's disciples.

What question did Paul ask them? (Acts 19:2)

_____

How did Paul describe the kind of baptizing John did? (Acts 19:4)

_____

_____

In what name did these believers then wish to be baptized? (Acts 19:5)

_____

_____

After they were baptized, Paul laid his hands on them.

What happened to them when Paul prayed for them? (Acts 19:6)

1. _____

2. _____

3. _____

5. John and Jesus

Having left the wilderness, John was preaching and baptizing in the Jordan River.

What did John call the Pharisees and Sadducees who showed up at his baptismal service? (Matthew 3:7)

_____

_____

He told the people he was baptizing them "for repentance," but the Messiah would offer them a different kind of baptism.

With what would Jesus baptize His followers? (Matthew 3:11)

1. _____

2. _____

When Jesus appeared at the Jordan River where John was baptizing, John immediately recognized him as the Messiah. Jesus then entered the water where John was baptizing.

Why had Jesus come to John? (Matthew 3:13)

_____

_____

What was John's response? (Matthew 3:14)

_____

_____

After baptizing Jesus, John continued his ministry of calling people to repentance. No doubt, since he had recognized Jesus as the Messiah, he had a great influence in pointing people toward the miracle-worker. John did not limit himself to the Jordan Valley, but traveled as far away as Samaria, in the Jezreel Valley in central Israel. Here he continued to baptize people. Some of the people asked him questions about Jesus.

What did John say about Jesus and about himself? (John 3:30)

_____

_____

What did John say would happen to those who believe in the Son of God? (John 3:36)

_____

What did John say would happened to those who reject the Son of God? (John 3:36)

_____

Herod Antipas, the ruler of Galilee and also Perea, a district east of the Jordan where John had begun his ministry, became alarmed that John's influence might breed a new rebellion among the Jews. Then John did something that angered Herod so greatly he had John arrested.

Why did Herod have John arrested and put in prison? (Mark 6:17-18)

_____

_____

_____

While John was in prison in the remote fortress of Machaerus on the eastern cliffs above the Dead Sea, he began to doubt if Jesus was really the Messiah. Perhaps he hoped Jesus would lead a rebellion against the Romans, or the puppet kings. Perhaps he did not understand why Jesus did not baptize as he had. Perhaps he wondered why Jesus did not renounce Herod, the Romans, and others. Maybe, knowing his days were numbered and feeling terribly lonely in prison, he was just discouraged.

What was John's question of Jesus? (Matthew 11:2-3)

_____

_____

Jesus told the messengers to go back to John and list the miracles Jesus was performing.

What were these miracles? (Matthew 11:5)

1. _____

2. _____

3. _____

4. _____

5. _____

6. _____

Jesus then encouraged John by saying that, even though their two ministries were vastly different, John would be blessed if he did not "fall away" because Jesus didn't meet his expectations. He then turned to the crowd and commended John as a man.

What did Jesus say about John's greatness? (Matthew 11:11)

_____

_____

The people believed that, before the Messiah would come, a certain prophet would reappear.

What did Jesus call John the Baptist? (Matthew 11:14)

_____

Jesus, however, pointed out that even though John was perhaps the greatest of all the prophets since he had actually introduced the Son of God to the world he was no greater than any other man when it came to salvation—that even the least in the Kingdom was greater than he.

John was finally executed on Herod's birthday. Herod's decree was egged on by his wife—who was also his sister-in-law—whom John had denounced.

What was the name of Herod's illicit wife? (Mark 6:17)

_____ Salome

_____ Jezebel

_____ Bathsheba

_____ Delilah

_____ Herodias

How did she feel about John the Baptist? (Mark 6:19)

_____

_____

How did Herod feel about John? (Mark 6:20)

_____

_____

_____

_____

What public promise did Herod make to the daughter of his wife when she danced before him and his military leaders? (Mark 6:22-23)

_____

_____

_____

_____

What did the girl do? (Mark 6:24)

_____

What did Herodias tell her to ask for? (Mark 6:24)

_____ Half of her step-father's kingdom.

_____ The head of John the Baptist.

What did the weak king do? (Mark 6:26-28)

_____

_____

_____

_____

WRAP UP

John was a man like us. At times he was bold. At other times he was filled with despair. Yet at heart he was a man of integrity. He had the courage to proclaim that Jesus was the Messiah. He also had the courage to denounce evil and injustice, knowing it could cost him his life. His mission was vastly different from the ministry of the One he came to introduce—but he was faithful. He paved the way for the Messiah and was therefore, even though a man like us, the greatest of the prophets.

FINAL LESSON

God honored John because John recognized that in order for Jesus to increase, he needed to decrease.

PERSONAL REVIEW QUESTIONS

Circle T (true) or F (false)

1. T   F   John was 40 years older than Jesus.

2. T   F   John's mother was Salome.

3. T   F   John's father thought John would grow up to be the Messiah.

4. T   F   Like the ancient prophets, John called people to repent.

5. T   F   When John saw Jesus at the Jordan he called him the "lamb of God."

6. T   F   John taught Jesus to baptize people.

7. T   F   Jesus baptized many people but told His disciples to "tell no man."

8. T   F   Jesus told His disciples to baptize people so they could take the Lord's Supper in church.

9. T   F   Paul called water baptism spiritual crucifixion.

10. T   F   John said Jesus would baptize people in the Holy Spirit.

11. T   F   Herod had John arrested because John rebuked him for marrying his sister-in-law.

12. T   F   Jesus said John was the greatest of the prophets.

MEMORY VERSE

John 3:30 (Memorize, then write it on these lines)

_____

_____

TRUE OR FALSE ANSWERS:

1-F, 2-F, 3-F, 4-T, 5-T, 6-F, 7-F, 8-F, 9-T, 10-T, 11-T, 12-T

NOTES

Lesson 8
Mary & Elizabeth
Yielded to God's Will

SCRIPTURE: Luke 1:26-56
VIDEO REFERENCE: Lesson #8
SUPPLEMENTARY READING REFERENCE:
  Ten Bible People Like Me
  Chapter VIII: "Mary & Elizabeth: Yielded to God's Will"

Introduction

No character in history—man or woman—evokes as much love and devotion from Christians as Mary, the mother of Jesus. She remains the greatest woman of all time. Yet she was a woman just like us. Young, frightened, confused— yet totally yielded to God's will for her life.

1. The Genealogies

Mary's place in history goes all the way back to Moses when certain laws were set in place by God to prepare the world for the coming of His Son. As a ruler and judge, Moses delivered thousands of judgments. Very few are mentioned specifically. One, however, takes on great significance.

A man by the name of Zelophehad, who belonged to the tribe of Manasseh, had died—leaving no sons to inherit his name or his property, as was the custom of the day. His five daughters came to Moses with a complaint.

What was the complaint of the daughters of Zelophehad? (Numbers 27:4)

_____

_____

_____

Out of this simple case God gave the nation of Israel a new law which would set the foundation for the coming Messiah—1200 years in the future.

If a man died and left no son, who received the inheritance? (Numbers 27:8)

If a man died and left no son or daughter, who received the inheritance? (Numbers 27:9)

_____

If a man died and left no sons, daughters, or brothers, who received the inheritance? (Numbers 27:10)

_____

If a man died and left no sons, daughters, brothers, or uncles, who received the inheritance? (Numbers 27:11)

_____

This obscure Old Testament law determines that daughters who want to inherit their father's property should marry within their tribe—because the intent of God was that property should remain in the tribe. However, the law meant more. It enabled Jesus, as the son of Mary, to be "King of the Jews." That is the purpose of these seemingly dull genealogies at the beginning of Matthew and Luke. It was important for the Jews to know that the Messiah was born according to the law and the Scriptures. Anyone claiming to be the Messiah, but not fulfilling the letter of the law, would be an imposter. In order for Jesus (who was legally considered Joseph's son) to inherit Judah's throne, Mary, who came from the tribe of Judah, had to marry within the same tribe.

Matthew proves this in his lengthy genealogy, tracing Joseph all the way back to Judah (Matthew 1:3).

Who does Matthew say was Joseph's father? (Matthew 1:16)

_____

Now we find a seeming contradiction in the Bible.

Who does Luke say was Joseph's father? (Luke 3:23)

_____

Actually, Heli was Mary's father. Joseph is called his son because he was Mary's husband and Heli's legal heir in the absence of any brothers of Mary. (The word "begat" or "father of" is not used in Luke.) Thus Luke, like Matthew, goes to great pains to prove that Jesus was legally from the tribe of Judah on Mary's side (Luke 3:33).

2. The Virgin Birth

Once it was determined that both Mary, Jesus' natural mother, and Joseph, Jesus' step-father (but declared by the authorities as his "legal" father), were of the tribe of Judah, the stage was set for the most magnificent event of history: the virgin birth.

What was Isaiah's prophecy 700 years earlier? (Isaiah 7:14)

_____

What was the child of this virgin birth to be called? (Isaiah 7:14)

_____

What does Immanuel mean? (Matthew 1:23)

_____

3. Mary

What was Mary's relationship with Joseph before Jesus was born? (Matthew 1:18, Luke 1:27)

_____

Mary was engaged (or betrothed) to Joseph. In the time of Jesus, engagements were a legal, binding relationship lasting one year. The only way an engagement could be broken was by a legal divorce. During the engagement (or espousal), the "husband" and "wife" lived separately and were not permitted to have sexual relations. After the year's engagement, a wedding was held, at which time the husband and wife were allowed to live together.

It was early on in this engagement that God sent an angel to deliver a message to Mary.

What was the name of the angel? (Luke 1:26)

_____ Michael

_____ Gabriel

_____ Lucifer

Who had chosen Mary for this task? (Luke 1:30)

_____

What was the angel's message to Mary? (Luke 1:31)

_____

_____

It was the most stunning message any human had ever received from God. Mary's question to the angel was natural.

What did Mary ask the angel? (Luke 1:34)

_____

_____

How was Mary to become pregnant? (Luke 1:35)

_____

If a virgin was to have a baby, which was conceived by the Holy Spirit, whose Son would the child be on His father's side? (Luke 1:35)

_____

To prove that he was from God, the angel then told Mary something that she did not know, but needed to check out.

What did the angel tell Mary? (Luke 1:36)

_____

What was Mary's response? (Luke 1:38)

_____

_____

4. **Elizabeth**

Elizabeth is described as a "relative," "kinswoman," and "cousin" of Mary. Some Bible scholars believe she may have been Mary's sister or step-sister. Her exact relationship with Mary is unknown, although it is obvious she and Mary were far more than distant relatives. She is described as "well along in years," a phrase which generally meant she was beyond the normal age of child-bearing. She and her husband, a priest, lived in the little village of Ein Karem, meaning "spring of the vineyard." This was a suburb of Jerusalem, a 90-mile walk from Mary's home.

Where did Mary live? (Luke 1:26)

_____ Bethlehem

_____ Nazareth

_____ Capernaum

What was the name of Elizabeth's husband? (Luke 1:5)

_____

Zechariah, who was a Levite (a descendent of Aaron and therefore a priest), was scheduled to minister to the Lord in the temple in Jerusalem. This was a high honor, something that might happen only once in a lifetime. When his great day came, he went with a heart prepared to meet God. Instead, God met him and granted him the desire of his heart.

Elizabeth and Zechariah had yearned for a child, but it seemed the time was past for that to happen. That day, in the temple, Zechariah was visited by an angel.

What was the angel's name? (Luke 1:19)

_____

What was the angel's message to Zechariah? (Luke 1:13)

_____

When was John to be filled with the Holy Spirit? (Luke 1:15)

_____ When he was baptized by Jesus in the Jordan River

_____ When the elders laid hands on him and prayed

_____ After he had been confirmed by the bishop

_____ From the moment he was born

_____ As soon as he was born again

What was Zechariah's reaction to the angel's announcement that his wife was to have a son in her old age? (Luke 1:18)

_____ Joy

_____ Doubt

_____ Grief

_____ Anger

What did Gabriel say would happen to Zechariah since he doubted God's message? (Luke 1:20)

_____ He would lose the ability to speak for the rest of his life

_____ He would lose the ability to speak until the baby was born

_____ He would be struck deaf and dumb

What was Elizbeth's reaction when she discovered she was pregnant? (Luke 1:25)

_____

_____

5. Mary and Elizabeth

After her visit from Gabriel, Mary immediately set out to visit Elizabeth, traveling the 90 miles from Nazareth to Jerusalem either on foot or riding a small donkey. She probably did not tell Joseph about the angel's visit until after she returned from visiting Elizabeth and was certain she was pregnant.

How far along was Elizabeth in her pregnancy when Mary arrived at her house? (Luke 1:24-26, 39)

Mary doubtlessly stayed on with Elizabeth until the baby was born before returning to Nazareth.

How long did Mary stay? (Luke 1:56)

What happened to Elizabeth when Mary greeted her? (Luke 1:41)

What did Elizabeth's unborn baby do when his mother heard Mary's voice? (Luke 1:41)

From the moment Elizabeth saw Mary, even before she heard Mary's story of the visit from the angel, she knew that God had touched Mary in a special way.

What did Elizabeth say to Mary? (Luke 1:42)

What title did Elizabeth call Mary? (Luke 1:43)

WRAP UP

No one knows exactly where the Messiah was conceived. Gabriel's announcement to Mary was in the future tense—"You will be with child. . ." (Luke 1:31). Elizabeth told Mary she was blessed because she believed that what the Lord had said "will be accomplished" (also future tense). There is reason, therefore, to believe the conception of the Messiah probably took place in Ein Karem. Mary then sang a magnificent psalm, known from its first word in the Latin version as the Magnificat, which reveals her choice character.

FINAL LESSON

Two women: Elizabeth and Mary. One old, one young. One to give birth to a prophet, the other to give birth to the Messiah. Both women would suffer the agony of birth. Both would know the intense pain and grief of losing a son. But both were chosen of God. Both were yielded to His will.

PERSONAL REVIEW QUESTIONS

Circle T (true) or F (false)

1. T F Mary came from the tribe of Levi.

2. T F The genealogies have no useful purpose in the Bible.

3. T F Joseph was known as Jesus' legal father.

4. T F The virgin birth is a myth.

5. T F Isaiah said the Messiah would be called Immanuel.

6. T F Isaiah said the Messiah would be born to a virgin.

7. T F Immanuel means "the glory of God has departed."

8. T F Mary was engaged but not married when she conceived.

9. T F The angel who came to Mary told her Elizabeth was pregnant.

10. T F John was filled with the Holy Spirit before he was born.

11. T F John jumped in his mother's womb when his mother heard the angel say Mary was coming to see them.

12. T F Zechariah called Mary "the mother of our Lord."

13. T F Elizabeth was a priestess in the temple.

14. T F The same angel that spoke to Zechariah also spoke to Mary.

MEMORY VERSE

Luke 1:37 (Memorize, then write it on these lines.)

_____

_____

TRUE OR FALSE ANSWERS:

1-F, 2-F, 3-T, 4-F, 5-T, 6-T, 7-F, 8-T, 9-T, 10-F, 11-F, 12-F, 13-F, 14-T

NOTES

Lesson 9
John Mark
Losers Can be Winners, Too

SCRIPTURE: Mark 14:51-52
VIDEO REFERENCE: Lesson #9
SUPPLEMENTARY READING REFERENCE:
  Ten Bible People Like Me
  Chapter IX: "John Mark: Losers Can be Winners, Too"

Introduction

The Bible is filled with stories of men who failed but were never classified as failures. All the people of the Bible were humans like us. They doubted God. They disappointed Him as well as each other. They failed time and time again. In this session we study the life of one of the greatest failures of the New Testament—yet he also became one of the true heroes of the faith.

1. Mark and Jesus

The night before Jesus was crucified, He gathered His twelve disciples into an upper room in Jerusalem. It was the Feast of the Passover. Following the Seder meal, Jesus took the remains of the bread and wine and passed them to His disciples. He then made a prediction.

What did Jesus tell His disciples? (Mark 14:27)

_____

Who immediately argued that even if the rest left Jesus, he would never fall away? (Mark 14:29)

_____

What did Peter insist emphatically? (Mark 14:31)

_____

_____

Later that night, the disciples followed Jesus through the dark streets of Jerusalem. They left the city through the Essene Gate and passed through the Kidron Valley. Climbing part way up the Mount of Olives, Jesus stopped in an old garden called Gethsemane.

What did Jesus ask His disciples to do? (Mark 14:32)

_____

Taking Peter, James, and John, Jesus went into an old olive grove. Expressing His anguish, He then asked them to do something specific.

What did Jesus ask them to do? (Matthew 26:38)

_____

Jesus then went into the olive grove to pray. Three times He returned, only to find the three disciples sleeping.

What did Jesus ask Peter when He wakened him? (Mark 14:37)

_____

_____

Suddenly there was a great commotion. Roman soldiers, led by Judas, one of Jesus' disciples, had come to arrest Him. Peter drew his sword to fight, but Jesus stopped him, saying He was being arrested to fulfill scripture.

Then what did all the disciples do? (Mark 14:50)

_____

It's at this point we meet, for the first time, young John Mark. A teenager, Mark had once considered joining the Zealots, a group of militant activists who advocated violent overthrow of the Roman oppressors. Then he met Jesus—perhaps through his friendship with Simon the Zealot or through Peter. There were a number of people who followed Jesus but were not part of the inner circle of the twelve disciples. Some were women: Mary, Martha, Mary Magdalene, Joanna. Some, like John Mark, simply wanted to be as close to Him as they could. Mark had joined the group as they left the Upper Room and was with the disciples when Jesus was arrested.

When the disciples fled, Mark was left behind. One of the Roman soldiers spotted him and grabbed him by his linen garment.

What did the young man do? (Mark 14:52)

_____

2. Mark and Barnabas

After fleeing into the dark, Mark disappears from history. Branded as a deserter, a coward—stripped of his garment as well as his self-respect—he has all the aspects of a failure. Mark, of course, was not the only one who fled that night. All those other "brave" disciples, including Peter who had vowed to die with Jesus, also turned tail and ran. However, after Jesus' resurrection, something had happened to change these bragging cowards into real men of faith and strength.

What had happened to Peter and the other disciples to change their lives? (Acts 2:1-4)

_____

_____

_____

It is probable that Mark was with the 120 on the day of Pentecost. However, he does not reappear in the pages of the New Testament for 15 years.

Persecution in Jerusalem was becoming intense. James, the brother of John, had been executed by Herod. Herod then had Peter arrested, intending to kill him. However, the night before Peter was to be tried and executed, an angel opened the prison doors and Peter walked out.

Where did Peter go when he left prison? (Acts 12:12)

_____

What was Mark's relationship to Barnabas, a leader in the Jerusalem church? (Colossians 4:10)

_____

While this was going on in Jerusalem, the church was growing in Antioch, Syria. Some of the refugees of the persecution which followed the death of Stephen had taken the lead in preaching to the Gentiles. Large numbers had accepted Jesus as Lord. The Jerusalem church sent Barnabas to oversee the ministry. Barnabas went to Tarsus to enlist the help of Saul (later called Paul). Both of them stayed in Antioch for a year as the church grew.

When Barnabas and Saul finished their mission, who did they ask to join them? (Acts 12:25)

_____   _____

3. Mark and Paul

Shortly afterwards, the church at Antioch sent out Barnabas and Saul as the first foreign missionaries. (By this time Saul's name had been changed to Paul.) Despite John Mark's earlier failures, they decided to give him a chance and took him with them. Luke, the physician, who was also keeping extensive journals, was along, too.

Where was their first stop after leaving the mainland? (Acts 13:4)

_____   _____

What was John Mark's job on the mission team? (Acts 13:5)

_____ Business manager

_____ Bodyguard to Paul

_____ Song leader

_____ Public relations and media expert

_____ Youth worker

_____ In charge of the puppet ministry

_____ Helper

In Pamphylia, Paul said it was time to head inland, through the back regions of Turkey, up into the high hills and tablelands to the cities of Asia Minor. It was going to be tough. The country was filled with thieves and cutthroats.

What did Mark do when the mission team headed inland? (Acts 13:13)

_____   _____

Mark's desertion in the face of fire must have been a huge disappointment to his older cousin, Barnabas, who had persuaded Paul to take him along. Paul no doubt saw Mark as a spoiled brat. His family had money (they had a big house in Jerusalem with servants), and Paul felt Mark was not tough enough to stick it out.

Who suggested that Paul take Mark along on the second missionary journey? (Acts 15:36-37)

_____

Why did Paul refuse? (Acts 15:38)

_____

_____

What happened between Paul and Barnabas? (Acts 15:39)

_____

_____

What did Barnabas do? (Acts 15:39)

_____

_____

Who did Paul choose as his traveling companion? (Acts 15:40)

_____ Peter

_____ Simon the Magician

_____ Lydia

_____ Aquila and Priscilla

_____ Silas

4. Mark and Peter

Only Barnabas, it seems, had any confidence left in Mark. At the age of 32, Mark had failed three times. Ten more years pass and we hear nothing of Mark. Then a letter makes the rounds of the various churches. It is from Peter, who is also travelling as a missionary.

Who is now traveling with Peter? (I Peter 5:12)

_____ Paul

_____ Barnabas

_____ Timothy

_____ Silas

Who else is traveling with Peter? (I Peter 5:13)

_____

Peter, who was also a failure in those early days, has reached out to Mark.

How does Peter describe Mark? (I Peter 5:13)

_____

During this time with Peter, Mark interviews him extensively for a book he is writing. It still bears his name and is included as the second book of the New Testament. It is the first biography ever written of Jesus Christ. Mark is no longer a loser. He has become a winner.

There are two more references to John Mark. Paul, now in prison in Rome awaiting execution for preaching the Gospel, has had a change of heart. Maybe it's because he finally saw in Mark what Barnabas and Peter saw in him. Or, perhaps Mark has changed. Whatever, he's no longer a coward, a failure, a loser. Now he's willing to die for his faith.

Who is also in prison with Paul in Rome? (Colossians 4:10)

_____

In what may have been his final letter, Paul writes his friend, Timothy. He is still in prison. Obviously, Mark has been released. But Mark is no longer the old deserter. Demas had deserted—gone back into the world. Crescens, Titus and Tychicus are in ministry. Only Luke is with Paul in prison.

Who does Paul ask to be with him in his last hours? (II Timothy 4:11)

_____

5. **Mark and Perseverance**

   What happens when a man of God stumbles? (Psalm 37:24)

_____

   Why will he not fall? (Psalm 37:24)

_____

   Who does Jesus say will be saved? (Matthew 24:13)

_____

Who are Jesus' disciples? (John 8:31)

_____

Even if trouble, hardship, persecution, famine, nakedness, danger, or sword comes our way, who are we in God's sight? (Romans 8:37)

_____

What can separate us from the love of Christ? (Romans 8:38-39)

_____ death

_____ life

_____ angels

_____ demons

_____ present

_____ future

_____ powers

_____ height

_____ depth

_____ all the above

_____ nothing

What does Paul tell us to do in troubled times? (I Corinthians 15:58)

1. _____

2. _____

3. _____

Who reaps the spiritual harvest? (Galatians 6:9)

_____ Those with great faith

_____ Those who never doubt

_____ Those who do not become weary in doing good

_____ Those who do not give up

_____ Those with lots of money

When we have done everything we know to do, what else should we do? (Ephesians 6:13)

_____

Who will keep us in the last day? (II Timothy 1:12)

_____

WRAP UP

The lesson of Mark, a man like us, can be summed up in an old adage: "If at first you don't succeed, try, try again."

FINAL LESSON

Losers are always winners as long as they never quit.

PERSONAL REVIEW QUESTIONS

Circle T (true) or F (false)

1. T F Peter was able to live up to his boast that he would not desert Jesus in tough times.

2. T F When Jesus was arrested, all His friends fled.

3. T F Jesus was betrayed by one of His own disciples.

4. T F John Mark was the only one to stand with Jesus when He was arrested.

5. T F God is impatient with people who fail.

6. T F God's people are often impatient with people who fail.

7. T F Paul refused to take Mark with him on his second missionary journey because Mark chickened out the first time.

8. T F Barnabas saw something in Mark Paul didn't see.

9. T F Paul finally came around and regarded Mark as a worthy minister.

10. T F God blessed Mark because Barnabas stuck with him.

11. T F God blessed Mark because Mark was willing to try again.

12. T F God does not require us to win, He just wants us to be faithful, do our best, and keep trying.

MEMORY VERSE

Philippians 1:6 (Memorize, then write it on these lines.)

_____

_____

_____

_____

TRUE OR FALSE ANSWERS:

1-F, 2-T, 3-T, 4-F, 5-F, 6-T, 7-T, 8-T, 9-T, 10-T, 11-T, 12-T

NOTES

Lesson 10
Simon Peter
Hearing God

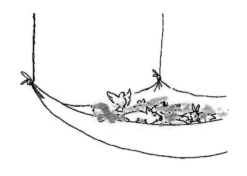

SCRIPTURE: Matthew 16:13-20
VIDEO REFERENCE: Lesson #10
SUPPLEMENTARY READING REFERENCE:
    Ten Bible People Like Me
    Chapter X: "Peter: Hearing God"

1. Hearing God

Hearing God correctly is one of the major problems facing all Christians. One part of the problem is hearing anything at all. The other part is discerning whether the voice you hear is God—or some other voice such as self, Satan, or just another man's advice.

Peter was a man like us. As a Jew he had been trained to believe God spoke once, from Mt. Sinai, and what He said was recorded in the Law of Moses. He may have spoken also through the prophets. While the Jews considered the Law inerrant, they considered the prophets merely inspired. The idea of God speaking today was foreign to them.

How did the writer of Hebrews say God had spoken? (Hebrews 1:1-2)

In the past: _____

In the present: _____

How did the prophet Joel say God would speak when the Holy Spirit was poured out on all people? (Joel 2:28)

Through sons and daughters: _____

Through old men: _____

Through young men: _____

In the days of Moses the Law was written on stone tablets.

Where did God say He would put and write the new law? (Jeremiah 31:33)

In their _____ .

On their _____ .

2. Speaking for God

With the coming of the Holy Spirit the gift of prophecy was given to the church.

What is prophecy? (II Peter 1:21)

_____

What gift did Paul say we should especially desire? (I Corinthians 14:1)

_____

When men prophesy what do they speak to men for? (I Corinthians 14:3)

1. _____

2. _____

3. _____

3. Revelation Knowledge

Peter was a prophet in that he heard from God. The first time he received "revelation knowledge" was at Caesarea Philippi. Jesus had taken His disciples north into Gentile country to this stronghold of all the ancient gods of Syria, Greece, and Rome. Here, in this dramatic setting, He asked them the first of two world-changing questions.

What was the first question Jesus asked His disciples? (Matthew 16:13)

_____

Who did they say others thought He was? (Matthew 16:14)
(Check correct answers.)

_____ Elijah

_____ Moses

_____ Abraham

_____ Adam

_____ Jeremiah

_____ John the Baptist

_____ An angel

_____ One of the prophets

What was the second question Jesus asked His disciples? (Matthew 16:15)

_____

How did Peter answer? (Matthew 16:16)

_____

Where did Jesus tell him the answer came from? (Matthew 16:17)

_____

Earlier, Jesus had told Simon he would one day receive a new name meaning "rock." At that time He used the Aramaic name.

What was the name Jesus said Simon the fisherman would be given? (John 1:42)

_____ Paul

_____ Samuel

_____ Judah

_____ Cephas

At Caesarea Philippi, Jesus tells Simon he is ready for his new name. This time He uses the Greek name for rock.

What did Jesus name Simon? (Matthew 16:18)

_____

Jesus said His church would be built on those who are able to receive revelation knowledge about His Lordship—who confess that Jesus is the Son of God and hear God daily through the power of the Holy Spirit.

4. Confessions of Others

While Peter was among the first to receive revelation knowledge that Jesus was the Messiah, others had heard God also.

Who did John the Baptist say Jesus was? (John 1:29)

_____

_____

What did John see and testify? (John 1:34)

_____

What did the demons call Jesus? (Mark 5:7)

_____

Whom did Simeon know he was to see before he died? (Luke 2:26)

_____

Did this come to pass? (Luke 2:28-30)

_____ Yes

_____ No

Whom did Andrew tell Peter he had found? (John 1:41)

_____

Who did the woman at the well tell others Jesus was? (John 4:29)

_____

5. The Confession of Jesus

There are those who say Jesus never declared, personally, that He was the Son of God.

Who did He tell His disciples He was? (John 10:30)

_____

How did Jesus say we were to honor Him? (John 5:23)

_____

Whom did Jesus say we see when we see Him? (John 12:45)

_____

What did Jesus tell the woman at the well? (John 4:26)

_____

What did Jesus tell the man He had just healed from blindness who wanted to know who the Messiah was? (John 9:35-37)

_____

What did He tell His disciples about His relationship with the Father? (John 14:9)

_____

When Thomas (a disciple who doubted that Jesus had been raised from the dead) met Jesus after the resurrection, what did he exclaim? (John 20:28)

_____

Did Jesus rebuke him for calling Him God? (John 20:29)

_____ Yes

_____ No

What did Jesus' enemies say He called Himself? (John 10:33)

_____

What did the high priest ask Jesus? (Matthew 26:63)

_____
_____
_____

What did Jesus answer the high priest? (Matthew 26:64)

_____

_____

_____

_____

Did the high priest doubt that Jesus had said He was the Son of God? (Matthew 26:65)

_____ He wasn't sure.

_____ He knew exactly what Jesus said.

What did Jesus tell Pilate when asked if He were king (Messiah) of the Jews? (Luke 23:3)

_____

To whom did Jesus say all power in heaven and on earth was given? (Matthew 28:18)

_____

6. **Building the Church**

Jesus told Peter He would "build His church" on Peter's confession that Jesus was the Son of God.

What did Jesus tell His disciples would happen if men acknowledged in front of others that He was Lord? (Matthew 10:32)

_____

_____

What did Jesus say would happen if men disowned Him in front of others? (Matthew 10:33)

_____

_____

Paul said there were two elements necessary to be saved.

What must you do to be saved? (Romans 10:9-10)

1. _____

   _____

2. _____

   _____

Hearing God and confessing Jesus was a trait Peter used many times as he helped build the Church of Jesus Christ. After Jesus ascended to heaven, the Gospel spread rapidly, not only to the Jews, but also to the Gentile world. Some of the Jewish Christians were upset with this. They thought only Jews could receive the Messiah. One day Peter was resting on the housetop of his friend, Simon the tanner, in the seaport town of Joppa. As the prophet Joel had predicted would happen after the Holy Spirit came, God spoke to Peter though a vision.

What did Peter see in the vision? (Acts 10:11-12)

_____

_____

_____

_____

What did God tell him to do? (Acts 10:13)

_____

Peter could not understand how God could ask him, a Jew, to eat things the Law of Moses called unclean.

How did God respond? (Acts 10:15)

_____

_____

_____

While Peter was wondering what the vision meant, a group of Gentiles arrived downstairs asking for him. They said an angel had appeared to a Roman military officer—a Gentile named Cornelius—living up the coast at Caesarea. The angel had told Cornelius to send for Peter. Peter realized God had spoken to him through the vision, telling him he should carry the Gospel to the Gentiles as well as to the Jews.

What did Peter say when he arrived at the house of Cornelius? (Acts 10:28)

_____

_____

_____

As the Jews received the Holy Spirit at Pentecost, now God was pouring out His Spirit on the Gentiles for the first time.

What happened as Peter preached to the Gentiles? (Acts 10:44-46)

_____

_____

_____

_____

When the apostles and Jewish Christian leaders heard what had happened with Peter, they were upset and called him on the carpet. Peter told them how he had heard God, and what had happened when he obeyed God.

How did the leaders of the Jewish church respond? (Acts 11:18)

_____

_____

_____

WRAP UP

Because Peter was willing to hear God, the Gospel was not confined to the Jews alone, but now belonged to the entire world. Because Peter, a man like us, heard God and acted on what he heard, God is still building His church, and men and women everywhere are receiving revelation knowledge that Jesus is the Christ, the Son of the Living God.

FINAL LESSON

God wants us all filled with the Holy Spirit so we may hear His voice.

PERSONAL REVIEW QUESTIONS

Circle T (true) or F (false)

1. T   F   God wants only the church leaders to hear Him.

2. T   F   God said He would pour His Spirit out on Pentecostals and charismatics only.

3. T   F   God wants to write His law on the hearts of all men.

4. T   F   Prophecy is God speaking through us to others.

5.	T	F	Peter knew Jesus was the Messiah because he had memorized 300 verses of Scripture.
6.	T	F	Even demons know Jesus is the Messiah.
7.	T	F	Jesus never did call Himself the Messiah.
8.	T	F	We don't have to belong to a church to hear God.
9.	T	F	God's church is made up of men and women who hear God.
10.	T	F	Jesus said it's okay to be a secret disciple.
11.	T	F	Jesus said you don't have to tell others youa re a Believer as long as you live a good life.
12.	T	F	All we have to do to be saved is believe in our heart that Jesus is Lord.
13.	T	F	God said nothing He has made is unclean.

MEMORY VERSE

Romans 10:9-10 (Memorize, then write it on these lines.)

_____

_____

_____

_____

_____

_____

_____

TRUE OR FALSE ANSWERS:

1-F, 2-F, 3-T, 4-T, 5-F, 6-T, 7-F, 8-F, 9-T, 10-F, 11-F, 12-F, 13-T

ABOUT JAMIE BUCKINGHAM

A master story-teller and Bible teacher, Jamie Buckingham has delighted millions around the world both in person and in print.

He wrote more than 45 books, including biographies of some of this century's best known Christians, including Pat Robertson (*Shout It from the Housetops*), Corrie ten Boom (*Tramp for the Lord* and others), and Kathryn Kuhlman (*Daughter of Destiny, God Can Do it Again* and others). His other biographies include the national best seller *Run Baby Run* (with Nicky Cruz), *From Harper Valley to the Mountaintop* (with Jeannie C. Riley), and *O Happy Day* (the Happy Goodman Family Singers). Other books by Jamie Buckingham include *Risky Living*, *Into the Glory* (about the jungle aviator branch of Wycliffe Bible Translators); *Where Eagles Soar* (a sequel to *Risky Living*); *A Way Through the Wilderness*; and *Jesus World* (a novel). He also wrote *Power for Living*, a book sponsored by the Arthur DeMoss Foundation that was given away to millions of people worldwide and resulted in untold numbers of people coming to Christ.

Jamie was more than an author of books. He was an award-winning columnist for *Charisma Magazine* and served as Editor-in-Chief of *Ministries Today Magazine* until his death in February of 1992.

A popular conference speaker, he was recognized as one of America's foremost authorities on the Sinai and Israel. He wrote and produced more than 100 video teachings on location in the Holy Land.

As a distinguished Bible teacher with graduate degrees in English Literature and Theology, Jamie was respected among liturgical, evangelical, and Pentecostal Christians. He was a close friend and confidant of many key Christians of the late 20th century, including Oral Roberts, Billy Graham, Catherine Marshall, Jack Hayford, Bob Mumford, Kathryn Kuhlman, Corrie ten Boom, John Sherrill, Bill Bright, John Hagee, Pat Robertson, and many others.

Most importantly, Jamie was a husband, father, grandfather, and founding pastor of the Tabernacle Church, an interdenominational congregation in Melbourne, Florida, where he served for 25 years, pastoring and discipling followers of Christ. He lived in a rural area on the east coast of Florida on a family compound with his wife, Jackie, surrounded by five married children and 14 grandchildren.

For more information on Jamie Buckingham please visit www.JamieBuckinghamMinistries.com. Many of his books, columns, additional writings, video devotional series, and audio sermons can be found on this website, which is dedicated to preserving his life works.

You can also order Jamie's book *10 Bible People Like Me*, based on this workbook and video series.

For more of Jamie Buckingham's books, teachings and devotionals, or if you would like additional copies of this workbook, go to:

www.JamieBuckinghamMinistries.com

Other video devotionals by Jamie Buckingham include:

10 Parables of Jesus
10 Miracles of Jesus
Journey to Spiritual Maturity
Armed for Spiritual Warfare
50 Days Before Easter

Risky Living Ministries, Inc.

www.RLMin.com

Made in the USA
Middletown, DE
28 April 2022

64898811R00068